MY
RELENTLESS
LIFE

ANDRE ALEXSEN

M◯tivational PRESS®
LEADERS IN GLOBAL PUBLISHING

Published by Motivational Press, Inc.
1777 Aurora Road
Melbourne, Florida, 32935
www.MotivationalPress.com

Manufactured in the United States of America.

ISBN: 978-1-62865-557-5

CONTENTS

INTRODUCTION

MY LIFE HAS BEEN AN INCREDIBLE adventure. I have cheated death many times, be it caused by my own hands or from the many accidents I have encountered. During thirty-five years of my life, I have had experiences as a Hollywood stuntman, daredevil and previous substance and alcohol addict. My experiences and encounters range from living inside of a jail cell, surviving wild animal attacks, parachute malfunctions and horrific car wrecks, working with the world's most famous individuals and being diagnosed with a terminal cancer...I've been through it all!

By the grace of God, I am still alive to share my life's stories and encourage you to follow your own aspirations. It's never too late to become what you should have been. My purpose for this book is to encourage, and show you the roads that should be avoided, and should you find yourself down a path you no longer wish to take, how to get out.

At this stage in my life, I may not be what I want to be, but thank God I'm not what I used to be! I'd like to thank Jesus for pulling me out of the fire, tempering me, and sharpening me like a sword, to be used for His Kingdom and Glory.

> *Whether you think you can, or you think you can't, you are right*
>
> *- Henry Ford*

DEDICATIONS

THIS BOOK IS DEDICATED TO God, Family, Country The United States of America, Israel and our allied nations, our Military, Law Enforcement, ICE, Border Patrol, EMTs, Firemen, Patriots, Militias, and all our Veterans, past, present, and future, who fight selflessly for our freedoms and our safety (The Real Heroes). It's also dedicated to people around the world who stay "Relentless" and persistent to helping others and their dreams. If you are not one of these people, maybe you can be after reading this book.

This book is also dedicated to some of the greatest people and toughest men on this planet who have helped train me and believed in me, including my Grandma Prayer Warriors, Mileva Petrovitch and Mary West, the living legends Grand Master Sensei Gokor Chivichyan, Godfather of Grappling Uncle/Judo Gene Lebell, Sensei Benny "The Jet" Urqidez, Sensei Karen Darabedyan, Bob Wall, Sensei Santos Flaniken, Banning Sweatland- United States Marine Corp, top LE officer for Houston, TCOLE instructor, President of Emergency Operations Proving Grounds (EOPG) the top global emergency first responders tactical training in America, fight trainer Cleve Langdon, and Templar Commando Hugh Simpson aka Mr. Valentine.

Motivational Mentions: Randy Miller and Hayden Rosenaur (top animal trainers), President Donald J. Trump and the whole Trump family, Gen James "Mad Dog" Mattis aka Chaos, Gen John Kelly, Sarah Huckbee Sanders, Trey Gowdy, Gen Michel Flynn, Roma Downey and Mark Burnett, Harrison Ford, Don Rickles, Director/mentor James Cameron, Kevin Foley Photography, Pierce Brosnan, Robin Williams, Steve Dean, Fredrick Dean, the Dean family, the FSE Family, Tupac

Shakur, Kid Rock, Dwayne Johnson, Arnold Shwarzenegger, Judy Mora, Scarlet Mora Walker (Horses for Production), Wolfgang Puck, Director Walter Hill, Steven Spielberg, Clint Eastwood, Ron Howard, Dillon Aero and the whole Dillon Family, Slick (best Military Chopper Pilot), Dad Rae Williams, Brother Chief Master Sergeant Al Williams, co-host Christian Billings, military skydive instructor Mirko Sokol Djordjevic, Colin Dangaard of the Australian Stock Saddle Company, the late Hugh Hefner, Howard Fine Acting Studio, the NRA, Stunts Unlimited, Seal Teams 2 and 6, Air Force PJs, USMC, and Hayastan MMA, Radostina Peteva, Neil Cruickshank (15 Agency), Justin Sachs and the A-team at Motivational Press. I'd also like to thank all the pastors and churches that I've listened to and attended. To all the haters who tried to slow me down and mess me up... thank you! You just added fuel to my fire!

God bless our Charities, Ministries and giving back; a portion of book sales goes to Wounded Warrior Project, Coastal German Shepherd Rescue, Christian charities to help abandoned and abused children, and Calvary Apostolic Ministries by Dr. Joseph D'Allende.

Last, but certainly never least, I'd especially like to thank my dear wife Lina, who has been my training partner, dive buddy, skydive partner, best friend, best encourager, and love of my life. As for anyone else and all of my dear friends I haven't directly mentioned, and you all know who you are, know that I am grateful and thankful for you. There's a saying: "For I can see further now because I stand on the shoulders of Giants." You are all Giants in my life.

CHAPTER 1

S.W.A.T. WAS I THINKING?

IT'S 4 O' CLOCK PM ON A FRIDAY afternoon in Irvine, California at the Bank of America and I look down at my cell phone and see a message that reads "GET OUT OF THE BANK NOW." As I turn around and head for the door, an army of S.W.A.T. with helmets, bullet proof vests and AR15s surround me and start screaming at the top of their lungs, "GET ON THE GROUND! GET ON THE GROUND NOW!" I was actually in shock...that this did not happen to me sooner. You see, I just left two other banks before this and got the money successfully. It was greed and stupidity that got me busted that day.

The message on the cell phone came from the bank parking lot from my so-called partner, a crack dealer who we'll call "NY" for short, and another guy from Nigeria, who ran the credit card fraud scam. They thought they had it all figured out and assured me that no one had ever been busted for doing this before. They had a passport shop in LA where you could walk in; they would pull down a screen that would simulate the shade of the DMV, then proceed take a picture of you and manufacture a driver's license in the name of the person whose credit cards they had just got done stealing.

It was a sophisticated ring with fake cashier's checks, credit cards, IDs, the whole nine yards. The name of the game was cash advances, $5,000-$10,000. Hit and run. It would always be a different state to make sure we got a little more time. I was playing an out-of-state business man, who needed a cash advance on his credit card. I thought I would practice my acting between auditions on this one.

That day, the man from Nigeria was in a too big of a hurry as we hit the third bank. He didn't check to see if the credit card was called in stolen. That was his job. Idiot. At that point I knew I was going down and alone. You see, NY knew my family and where they all lived. It was time for me to take my medicine like a man. I was looking at three years to start.

When they arrested me and took me in, the interrogators grilled me for hours. I gave them nothing. My family's lives were on the line. Plus, it wasn't my first rodeo. I had been arrested many times before in almost every major police station from LA County, Orange County, Van Nuys, Hollywood, Ventura County, West Valley, Santa Monica/Venice, and yes, even Clark Country in Las Vegas, Nevada for DUIs, resisting arrest, and a high-speed pursuit in a stolen Porsche...so they say. Sort of a Tour De Jails, if you will, but never any crimes of violence against innocent people, except bar fights and jail riots; but those guys weren't innocent. I was a connoisseur of the un-fine dining completed with green baloney sandwiches and the so-called peanut butter and jelly with rotten apples on the side. But hey, do the crime, and you do the time.

I was locked up for days without telling them who I was. They brought in a top detective investigator known as "The Closer" (because they close the deal by any means possible), who tried to scare the shit out of me and that's par for course. If you knew anything about NY, top crack dealer in Compton/Inglewood and formerly from Brooklyn, he was the original Biggie Smalls and nobody to mess with. It was no joke, not to mention the scary Nigerian guy and his contacts. You would automatically know that your niece, your sister and your mom weren't safe if you even hinted that it wasn't you doing it alone. In fact, I was concerned that they might track the cell phone number back to them and bust them too. But that never happened, thank God!

I still gave them nothing. After reviewing all the tapes from all the banks and finger printing me again, they knew who I was. They walked in and said: "Ah, Mr. Alexsen. Back again, are you?" I replied: "Apparently so." It was too late and too stupid to deny any more after that.

After many extensions at the Newport Beach Courthouse, and about a year of going through a loser attorney and two useless public defenders, I got the bright idea to get a real attorney. The woman judge had had enough. It just so happened that the cases she hated the most were identity theft and credit card fraud. Bingo, I was the poster boy for that. So, when I made my plea that I was firing my public defender, she simply replied, "Bailiff, buy him a baloney sandwich downstairs." And to the innocent world that means hand cuff him, take him into custody and take him downstairs where all the other felons and criminals are.

Imagine if you will, me in a dress shirt, dress slacks, and dress shoes. I was taken downstairs, passing rows of packed jail cells of African Americans, Mexican Americans and other assorted gang members, all dressed in

Orange County Jail jump suits with lovely tattoos on their necks and tear drop tattoos under their eyes. The single teardrop signified that they had murdered someone already. The jeering shouts and whistles were all directed toward me from the packed cells. You see, these guys were already in different jails and prisons and had court dates that reoccurred in that same court. For that reason, they were locked up like caged animals…not in a good mood and awaiting their final ax to come down.

It was there that I had to lay my boundaries down, as one of the gang members yelled out, "Hey you look nice. Give me your shoes!" When I replied, "Come and take them, bitch," you could hear a choir of "Oooooohhhhhh" from the other inmates. He had been put in check in the meantime. I was pretty proud of myself until a big sheriff walked over and said to me, "You must be either really crazy or really bad-ass because if the judge finds you guilty, then you are boarding the bus with all of them this weekend."

That is how many people die on the bus. You see, you are chained to one inmate's wrist with only one hand to fight back. Upon the gang leader's cue, one of your wrists are held down while another gang member makes a fist with a #2 sharpened pencil and punches you in the esophagus, leaving the pencil there for you to die. The sheriffs can't reach you because they are all locked up in the front of the bus with shotguns, and you are in the back in a rolling cage with animals.

It was time to pray yet again. I had clearly heard God's voice tell me "No!" when this opportunity came up to make some fast cash with the lure of free crack, but I didn't listen. Now here I sat, alone in a cell, pondering my future state of health and wellbeing. I had been in jails before and could handle myself, but these boys were all gang members from Santa Ana; it wasn't one on one, and I had no backup!

The D.A.'s office had sent down a representative to ask me if I would take a deal for 16 months, 3 years' probation, a felony charge, and admission of guilt for all of my crimes. It had been dragging on long enough. In my mind I thought, "Don't gotta ask me twice," but to the D.A.'s office I said, "Well, ok," and asked if I needed to turn myself in today. The only negotiating chip I had was that if I took the plea, they would allow me one month to turn myself back in to get prepared for going away. And that was actually for ALL that I had done. A blessing. It was during a time when the jail cells were so over-crowded that even what I had done paled in comparison to murder, rape, drive-bys and major crack and meth dealers getting busted in Santa Ana, the uglier side of Orange County.

Well, I had one month to get my affairs in order. During that time, I was raising my first bangle tiger named Anastasia. She was about five months' old and getting kind of large. I knew that I couldn't keep her any longer, especially if I went away. I made arrangements to get her to Wild Life Way Station, and then on to Rocky Mountain Sanctuary, where they kept 11 tigers per 40 acres in Colorado in natural habitat surroundings.

I was sad, but it was the ideal situation and I had to do the right thing, knowing that one day I would get back to working with wild animals. I had done my first tiger rescue and conservation, whether I knew it at the time or not. Anastasia was sold out of a backyard with other tiger cubs by some people in the Middle East, who shouldn't have had them and they got busted. Oops.

I also had car payments to make and had lost my job, making it impossible to go to castings. So, I filed for unemployment, hid my car and turned myself in a month later. I refrained from telling anyone where I was going except, one person, my friend Linda. One hour prior to turning myself in, I bought a wife beater tank top and found a pair of lose baggy jeans with tennis shoes and a checkered Pendleton shirt. I slicked my hair back with some pomade, buttoned only the top button of the Pendleton and walked into court. Instant Gangster.

You have to understand, I had been in the joint before. Turning yourself in on a Friday night in to Men's Central Jail, going through two days of processing, and possibly waiting 24-48 hours before you even get betting and jail clothes - you need to be comfortable and ready to rumble. So, you got to fit in to avoid getting fucked with. It was a wise choice.

On the bus ride to the Men's Central Jail in Santa Ana, it was hot, dirty, crowded and edgy, and we hadn't even gotten to the jail yet. Upon arriving at the jail, we were handcuffed and shackled on our feet with chains. They then started to process us like so many of the cattle and criminals that we were. They started to put us into holding cells, which is all concrete with exposed toilet seats in the corner, most of them not working and flooding over.

You get into the cell as fast as you can and grab the first roll of toilet paper that you can get your hands on, if you are lucky. Two reasons. One reason is to lay your head down on the concrete floor because for hours on end, there is no place to sit and you want to at least put the roll under your head. Reason number two being that if someone wanted some toilet paper, rather than giving them the roll, you tear them off some squares and that's that.

It's Friday night, and as if the jails aren't crowded enough, here come the drunks and the drug addicts, just arrested in their street clothes. It's hot, humid and stinky, and here you have people yelling, fighting and throwing up in the corner. You would have had be there to know.

You start to meet people to pass the time away until they decide which final penitentiary they will put you in. One guy that I befriended I really felt sorry for. He was just a regular OC guy who had lost money in the stock market and real estate, and tried to make it up by selling illegal marijuana to keep his house. His wife divorced him, and his pride and joy was his 5-year-old daughter. He had bought a 12 gauge shotgun to protect himself for his new business. At some point, he had put his shotgun on his lap to check it out and it went off. He then realized that his daughter was no longer standing there next to him.

He saw the bottom of her feet sticking out of the closet he had just blown her into. He was highly distraught, and even once in emergency care, no one would talk to him or give him info on the status of his daughter. It was an accident, but he was going down for it nonetheless. I got on the payphone with my prayer warrior friend Paul because I needed it. When I got done speaking to Paul, I realized that this guy needed more prayer than me. Paul talked to him, prayed for him, and he received Jesus on the spot. The first of many to come.

Eventually, we were all separated and bussed to the facilities we were going to do time in. It was summer, and I remember because I got put in one of the oldest places with no air conditioning. Part of it was an old Army barracks and part of it was new, holding 1500 to 2000 inmates. Around that time, my mom had one of her first heart incidents; I bet what I did didn't help either. So there really was nobody to come visit me or put money on my books to buy things that I wanted. But hey, that's why they call it jail. It ain't supposed to be summer camp!

We got put into a large yard with guard towers, razor ribbon fencing, and it was the first place that you got put into when you arrived. Some people would call it "Hell" because it was the hottest and driest part of the facility, and it sure was that.

As soon as you got in, you had to join a car, otherwise known as a gang. There were the Chinos (Asians), the Bloods (Blacks) and the South Siders (Mexican American Chicanos). You also had the Mexican guys from Mexico who got caught in America and were called Pisa, and believe it or not, the South Siders and the Pisas did not get along. Then there was the Arian Brotherhood, us crazy white guys also known as "Pecker Woods," or "Woods" for short.

You had to belong to a car or a crew. You couldn't just stay to yourself and hope that everything was going to be ok. We had daily riots popping off instantly and you had to fight for your race. If you ran or hid, your race would find you and tax you; meaning beat the shit out of you for being a wuss and letting them down.

The white boys had to be crazier because there were less of us. We took that shit seriously with daily workouts and calisthenics, like some sort of crazed military unit counting out loud to make sure everyone noticed. Sometimes a car would tax their own member for doing something stupid, like stealing from another car and causing a riot, making us lose yard time; and what's worst is that the guards would charge in with tear gas, mace and clubs. When they were done with us, they would take all our commissary and letters from home, tear them up and put them in a big pile along with the garbage and pour either coffee or soda on top of the mess so nothing was retrievable. They did this to keep us in check.

I learned early on that segregation was very important there. An Arian, a shot caller who was the leader of that car taught me this. He asked me, "Why are you talking to that black guy for so long?" I told him I was sharing the Bible with him. He simply suggested that I shorten my sharing time and be careful.

I was then moved to the other side of the facility, where it was a lot better than where I was prior. Somehow, I was still unsettled. I got into a working cell block that ran the cafeteria and prepped the food. It was strange to see knives on 4-inch chains bolted to stainless steel tables. But you were glad they were!

Later, when my mom was in recovery, she was able to put money on my books and I got a little bit of commissary. A commissary is a sort of store where you can purchase your necessities from their list of items, such as toothpaste, snacks, ramen noodles, and the mother lode; the most valuable thing in jail that you take for granted - coffee. I remember coming back from working in the kitchen and noticed that my commissary bag of food had been stolen. I could have killed somebody for that, but I never found out who it was. It made me angry and bitter knowing that it was not going to get replaced and that I would have nothing.

Once more I was moved to what would be my final destination, Delta cell block. I came to find out that it was the best place you could be. This place had jobs in the barber shop, the library, and the warehouse. The warehouse was of most important because that was where all the new boots, new jeans, new clothes, and everything came from. When you first arrive, you get a bunch of old, stretched-out, nasty, used underwear and pants and old hobo looking boots that had one lace across the bottom, if you're lucky. This was a good place to stay to myself if I could; stay out of trouble and finish my time.

A big white guy named Lee ran the cell block; everybody liked Lee. He was a natural born leader who knew how to handle 150 men in that cell block and run it smoothly. Lee was to be released the next morning.

Smooth is preferred, so the sheriffs appreciated an inmate running the cell block. The last thing the sheriffs want to do is have to get up, come out of that "bubble" fortified glass enclosed octagon with metal doors, where they watch you with their riot gear on and miss their frickin' favorite TV show or Monday Night Football. Although I think some of the sheriffs actually enjoyed stomping on us.

Unfortunately, Lee had a problem. Somebody had stolen commissary from one of the South Siders, and it was suspected to be one of the Woods. By dawn for sure, you could expect a riot. Word would get passed on to the next cell block through a kite, which was a folded triangle shaped piece of paper that would be passed from one inmate to another through the cell block, coordinating the shot callers of each car that it was going to pop off in the morning and to be ready. Crude but efficient!

Lee had told me that he didn't want to go out that way and would bring out the news to the barracks in his last evening report. You see, at the end of every day, it was up to the cell block leader, aka "House Mouse," to address everyone and tell them what was going on.

I was still bitter from my stolen commissary, so I told Lee that I would be more than happy to speak. He said to the inmates on that evening report, "This is Andre. He's a new guy and he has something to say so listen." I stood up, and I don't know what got into me, but I made sure to get it out. I yelled and it echoed through the cell block, "HEY YOU. YOU LOW LIFE SCUMBAG BITCH." They all looked at each other like, who is he talking to? "YEAH YOU. YOU KNOW WHO I'M TALKING TO. YOU STEAL FROM ONE OF US WHILE WE ARE AT WORK? WE'RE GONNA FIND YOU AND WHEN WE DO, YOU WON'T GET A D.A. OR A JUDGE, JURY, OR A FAIR TRIAL. YOU'LL JUST GET THE PUNISHMENT IN THE CORNER AND WE WILL ALL BEAT YOUR ASS FOR THIS." I remember walking away, not knowing what was going to happen. But as I listened, I heard one clap turn into 2, which turned into 10, and that turned into 100. I had then realized that it was a pretty fair statement for jail house justice.

I went to bed with my boots on that night. You see, you sleep with your boots on so when you gotta get up and fight, you're ready. It was about 5AM and I saw 5 guys standing over me at my bed, and I thought it was going be a blanket party, where they throw a blanket over you and start beating on you mercilessly. The leaders from each car started to shake me to wake me up, telling me that Lee was gone. They said, "Hey dog, you gotta run the cell block. After what you said last night, you're the one". I replied, "Uh, no. I just want to mind my own business, do my time, and get out of here."

They were pretty insistent, so eventually, I figured why not, thinking for sure that the sheriffs would say no. As I got up, I saw a long line of guys wanting to do the same and found out that it was actually a pretty solid job description. You get access to the phone, yard and TV, you get to stay in the barracks all day and run all stations, including the clothing warehouse, barbershop and library. Not bad.

I walked in to meet with the sheriffs and they asked me what I did. I told him I was a stuntman/actor. They Googled me, then proceeded to ask me why I was there, which they already knew. They were kind of smart asses, which I guess helped them pass the time. I told them that I would run the barracks like a business, or a corporation, with a couple of good officers at my side and things would be different. They told me to get out and called me back in 10 min later and said, "Alexsen, me and the other officers think that you would stink at this job." I then started for the door when they all laughed and said, "Just kidding. You got it." I got more than my bargain for it.

There are many perks to this job, however, it is very dangerous. Your duties were to come into the bubble, report to the sheriffs and clean out the bubble along with their trash, all the whole pretending like you were not friendly or giving them any info. Otherwise, the other inmates will call you a rat and kill you; and that could happen just on the word of gossip. Right or wrong, this was a dangerous position to be in!

My first order of business was to wake everyone up in the morning. The lights would turn on, and I would yell, "GET UP! LET'S GO! EVERYBODY UP!" I then had control of the supply closet where I would get out the hot water percolator. Coffee is a mandatory first thing in the morning in an ugly world. We would then stand in long lines and shave, and then get the boys off to work like some overgrown school kids. I was like a stepdad of some sorts to these criminals, yet I was one too, so it didn't make me any better to judge them. I decided to make the best of it and serve God, since not listening to Him was how I got there. I wanted to turn my life around.

It was then that I realized, "Wow, there's the payphone!" Usually, outside near the payphone was a constant huge line of people who would literally be fighting to get their phone time. But now, I got to use the payphone in the middle of the day while everyone else was at work. Since we didn't have money or change, you'd have to call collect, the operator would dial the number and the person you called would have to accept the charges. You could stab somebody with a shank, but God forbid that we have some quarters or dimes in our possession. Silly. I started clearing my many voicemails, probably 30-40, hearing about people starting to get mad because I wasn't calling them back. I was a little busy trying to stay alive!

My Grandma Betty from Texas had called and left a message after tracking me down through my friend, Linda. She had found one of Linda's modeling pictures online, Betty had never spoken to Linda, but knew she was my friend, and gotten the photographer's name off the bottom of the picture. She somehow found the photographer and got a hold of Linda, who figured it'd be ok to tell her where I was. My grandma is not very compute savvy, so it was a miracle that she was able to do that to find me. I gave my grandma a call back and she told me that I should have told her where I was, saying she wouldn't have judged me, but rather, she would have prayed for me.

My biological grandma, Mileva, had died while I was slipping and messing up on drugs. I was so regretful that I didn't have more time to spend with her, so I prayed to God that somehow, by some miracle, He would give me another Grandma. I really didn't know what I was asking at the time, but it's what I prayed for. Grandma Betty worked on the prayer line at John Hagee Ministries in San Antonio, Texas.

I would call the prayer line for years, while I was struggling with addiction and alcohol, and I would get this little old lady named Betty, who prayed for me all the time. One day I called, and Betty was gone. All the other old ladies on the prayer line knew me, and it was her friend Earlene that informed me that Betty was no longer working at the prayer rooms, but felt that it would be alright to give me her number. I called Betty on her personal line and she was so happy to hear from me. You see, it turns out that Betty never had kids or grandkids and lived alone. One day, the same moment that I had a question for her, she said, "I have a question for you." We simultaneously asked, "Will you be my Grandma/Grandson?" She's been like a real grandma ever since, and still is to me.

God answers the most obscure prayers. Don't think there's nothing you can't pray and ask for. It turns out we had so much in common. I was a cowboy and a Patriot who loved John Wayne movies, Westerns and Texas. It was befitting that I should get a little cowboy hat and boot wearing, fire cracker of a grandma named Grandma Betty.

Boy, did she teach me how to pray and become a prayer warrior! She encouraged me through some of the hardest times of my life. We talked to each other on the phone and sent pictures back and forth for 15 years but had never met in person. Finally, she came and lived with me for a while in my Spanish Western house in Lobo Canyon after I got married. She just had to meet my wife Lina. And they got so close. We had some great times. Anyway, I had received much needed prayer and I was at peace after I talked to Grandma Betty.

After the inmates got back from work, the first order of business that night was to warn everybody because the riot was still about to happen, and it was gonna happen on my watch. I announced to everybody to stay cool about the stolen commissary. I then took a bag of chips over to the South Sider who had been stolen from and put it on his rack, or bed. I looked on, amazed, as I saw inmates from different cars and colors walk

past his rack after me and give one item of commissary to keep the peace. It was a revelation for me.

The next day, while everyone was at work, I had the white guy that somebody had told me was the perpetrator, stealing the South Sider's food; a tweaker meth head by nature. I could make one of two choices, one being not to say anything, or turn him in and possibly get him killed. I prayed over it and wound up using a technicality that God gave me. The sheriffs had told me that if I ever feel that somebody's life is in danger, I should report it and they would remove them immediately, or else the blood would be on my hands if something happened. With that in mind, I reported him, and he was pulled out in the middle of the night. By the time everyone woke the next morning, his rack as empty and he was gone.

Where did he go? Back to the worst side of the facility, the place no one wanted to be when they first came in. Essentially, he lost his job, a good cell block to be in, and ended up sitting there and doing the rest of his time. That's when the term "Fed-Ex Man" was attached to me, because if you give me a problem, I'll ship you out overnight. I made a lot of enemies like this, but it kept the peace.

The next day I started to realize what a blessed spot I was in. I had no more commissary or any money that was going to be put on my books, but everyone else was going to pick up theirs. People were walking in with big paper bags stapled at the top, filled with candy bars, chips, pretzels, coffee, etc. I was pleasantly stunned when I saw the inmates opening their bags and throwing a bag of chips, a candy bar and other items from their commissary onto my rack, which was the first next to the door. I said to the shot callers, "What is this? What's up?" They said in their gangster way, "We gotta break some off for the house. You the house. You run the show. Its respect, dog."

I then got into what I was doing. I said ok, let's get some more yard time and get better movies. I started bringing guys to church and used the library to bring back Spanish and English Bibles. I was helping write court appeals for the guys; anything I could do to stay positive and busy. I would pray for people, preach to these guys, and I even got commissary for writing the guys' poems for their wives and sweethearts!

However, during that time, not all was well. There are 148 bad asses in there every day, with 3-4 released every night, and 3-4 new hard cases every morning. In response, I got myself a first officer named "Clint". An Ex-Marine Vet, a leader of the feared "La Mirada Punks" and former meth dealer. He was also a torpedo, or enforcer, for the Woods. You name your target, point him in that direction, and he does not stop till he destroys his objective or person. He watched my back and since he was from that area, he knew all the gangs, he had a reputation and he would get information that I couldn't; he was a good guy to have on my side.

As soon as somebody came in with a new bed roll under their arm, Clint and I would confront them, read them the rules of the house and tell them that if they screwed up, I would ship them out overnight. If they didn't want to comply with that, there was 148 men in my cell block that liked the way that it was, and they were ready to enforce it. I also told the shot callers of each car that instead of taxing their members, to give them to the house. They asked, "What does that mean?" I'd have them scrubbing the toilets and mopping the whole cell block, and that was more humiliating than getting a beating. But hey, they had a choice. Clean, or go to the other side. I had the cleanest cell block and the sheriffs were happy. The plan was working for the most part, but there are always speed bumps on a road.

I soon realized that there is nothing more important to these gang leaders and shot callers than to have new pressed jeans, new shiny boots, and new khaki denim shirts. Since I ran the warehouse, they got it. It was some sort of a status symbol in jail if you were clean and pressed looking. It's jail. I know, but it was also for their wives and sweethearts too. I was then called "The Juice Man". I asked them why. They said, ""Cause you got the juice. You got the power, man." I hadn't had anyone call me Andre for a long time. I had my hair slicked back and dark, looking like Vinnie from New York. Somehow, the rumor spread that I was some sort of hit man for the Mafia in New York and had somehow ended up there. I honestly don't know who started it, and it wasn't me, but I let it be!

Running a cell block is like running a bunch of deadly, dysfunctional, overgrown kids, so you either gotta step away, or lay the law down. One night, I got so angry and frustrated because we had it made and everything was going well, yet people were taking it for granted and slipping.

At the end of the day, I just threw up my hands and yelled, "FUCK IT. IF YOU ALL WANNA ACT LIKE BITCHES, IM DONE. I QUIT. THIS IS A WASTE OF TIME. I NO LONGER RUN THIS CELL BLOCK. I'M GONNA BE LIKE ONE OF YOU. AND MY NAME AINT JUICE MAN ANYMORE. IM THE CRAZY INMATE ON RACK #1, INMATE #01947." I took my shirt off, and I stormed back to my rack after saying, "AND IF ANY OF YOU WANNA FIND OUT ABOUT ME AND TEST ME I'LL BE WAITING ON ALL OF YOU. COME GET SOME."

I was a little bit shaky after that and I was ready, but I thanked God that nobody showed up except for a couple of inmates who approached me to calm me down. It was actually funny to see big crazy guys being humble in their own way, trying to say they're sorry.

So, it was some sort of Summer Holiday and the other inmates talked me into making jail made Pruno. What's that you ask? That's where every inmate at breakfast, lunch and dinner pockets packets of sugar and all of the fruit that they can. They then bring it to me and I put it in a big garbage bag, letting it sit for weeks, and its fermentation creates alcohol! How it works is the garbage bag fills up with air, you release the air, and it fills up a little bit less next time, and you keep releasing the air till there's no more air, and your vintage is ready. I kept it in a storage closet that only I had access to. Ah, August was a great month for Pruno. It was like the scene from *The Great Escape* where they made alcohol for 4th of July and I was Steve McQueen.

After the sheriffs went on their weekly rampage to find contraband from tobacco to meth to shanks (homemade knives and stabbing devices), and would tear up the cell block, I came up with an idea. I asked all the inmates to hand over 10% of all the contraband to me. They were more than happy to do it till I explained why. You see they said, "10% goes to the house anyway." and I replied, "Ain't that kind of party." I went to the sheriff's bubble and I handed it in anonymously. I told them that some of the shot callers and other inmates caught some guys and found this and we wanted to hand it in. You should have seen the look on their faces. It's the way a calf looks at a new gate. Huh? But, it worked. It relieved the pressure valve and we got more yard time, more movies, more everything. So, all were pleased, except for a few jealous people who always had their eye on killing me. Other than that, it was ok.

In addition to giving the inmates in the cell block daily updates, I got them to start praying. It was quite a sight. 148 men in a giant circle in front of their racks in their white T-shirts and underwear, repeating my prayers in unison. It was the Lord's Prayer every day, which went like this:

"Our Father in heaven, hallowed be Your name, Your Kingdom come, Your will be done on earth as it is in heaven. Give us today our daily bread. Forgive us our debts, as we also have forgiven our debtors. And lead us not into temptation, but deliver us from the evil one."

I would say a line, and they would repeat it. As we took prayer requests, our prayers got more and more powerful. The majority of inmates there were Latin and Spanish speakers, so in respect and to make sure I got through to everyone, I spoke the Lord's Prayer in Spanish as well. And they loved it. It helped transcend racial boundaries. 'Cause in God's eyes, all lives matter!

One night the sheriffs said to me, "What are you doing in there Alexsen, what's going on?" They tried to get me to chill out on that. So the next night, I prayed for the sheriffs and their families out loud. I swear, they were so loud, it felt like the windows were vibrating. But the sheriffs never said anything about my praying after that again. One of the inmates asked me, "Why are we praying for the sheriffs?" I replied, "'Cause God says to even pray for our enemies." He nodded and walked away.

It was at that stage of the game that the sheriffs and detectives had an offer for me, to possibly to shorten my sentence. A girl had been brutally murdered in Santa Ana and they suspected that it was one of the 1500 inmates. They wanted me to find out who. Now, if you had ever been to jail and on top of that, running a cell block, you know that asking those kind of questions is like asking for someone to stick a #2 pencil into your esophagus while you sleep. It's certain death if they find out. But I tried, not for them, but for God, and for the family of the girl who wanted closure.

It was a very high-risk situation. Because I was a trustee and considered safe, they had told me that they would pull me out of the cell block for a day to clean an office building off the facility. They were pretty smart about it when they decided to take a few guys along and not just me. But still, it made me paranoid. It didn't look good. During the cleaning of the office, I was pulled out and taken into one of the office rooms and briefed by the sheriffs on the homicide, which started me on a whole new career path later on in my life.

After accumulating as much info with some detective work, and formulating a subtle plan with the assistance of Clint, I narrowed it down to two guys. Now I don't judge people by their looks, but when I saw one of them, you could just feel the spirit of death around him. I gave the information to the sheriffs and they pulled in the suspects and interrogated each of them on time and dates, and found out that one of them was the guy. He was a South Sider that was actually bragging a little bit and trying to act badass by talking about some people that he killed.

After that, things started to feel very hot and uncomfortable for me. Maybe it was just me, but after sending so many guys back to "Hell," I had made a lot of enemies. I had been reminded by a Mexican guy that no matter how much power or juice I thought I had in that facility, the final say will always come down to the Mexican mafia, or La Eme, who ran the majority of the prisons; but the Arian Brotherhood would have something to say about that. I got what he was trying to tell me, even though this guy had gone to jail because he was high and while driving his car, a "voice" told him to punch on his gas pedal, crash through a gate, and run down all the head stones in a cemetery. I still found his words to be true.

At that point, two other inmates that entered the block threw everything that I was doing for a loop. One was a strange Albino. He didn't hang out with the Woods, and he talked with a South Sider accent, so he hung out with them. It was very strange and creepy to witness. From the first time I saw him, I knew there'd be big trouble. The second guy was an OG South Sider, meaning he's been around the system for a while. He was also a shot caller putting him high in the prison system ranking. He had a spider web tattoo on his neck and a tear drop tattoo under his eye. All the months that I had been there resolving the riots, helping guys get appeals, getting right with God, and receiving Jesus…all of that work was about to come to an end!

Things were getting threatening fast. In addition to the warehouse, barber shop and library, my crew was tasked with cleaning out the buses when they came from court to central jail. The sheriffs were pulling out my guys at 3 and 4 AM to clean the blood out of the buses because an unusually high amount was getting stabbed and killed. Whether in the jail or on the bus, they will get you; and the bus is easiest.

I also started to notice that somebody was starting to break into the cleaning closet where cleaning chemicals and bars of soap were missing. That may not seem like much, but bars of soap were put into pillow cases and swung as a weapon. Cleaning supplies will be poured down your throat and they hold you down till you die. At that point, there was an unusual number of South Siders in my cell block and they were starting to get more rebellious than normal. I knew the catalyst was the Albino guy.

One day he tried to start a fight, or a fake fight in the corner of the cell block and lured me there. As I tried to settle things down, I had quickly noticed that he got behind and to the side of me and was preparing to do something. At that point, everything was settled. I tried to have the sheriffs remove him and called him out as an instigator. They took him out for the day, and for the first time that I had ever seen, they brought him back in. I don't know what he said, or what his deal was with them, but he had been around institutions and jails since he was a kid and all he wanted was to start trouble all the time. He didn't want to be in a working cell block. He tried to cause a situation that would put him in some sort of a solitary confinement and he was ready to do anything to get what he wanted.

It was at 6AM when we got up, that somebody had told me that there was a green light out on me. Green light is marked for death, and anyone in the same car as the shot caller that called the green light was out to get me; that is a lot of people. I asked who it was and somebody had told me that it was the OG South Sider with the spider web and tear drop, who was friends with the Albino.

Now you're not supposed to throw a green light on anyone even if you are a shot caller, without higher appeal from a higher officer in the jail system. But I wasn't going to hang on that technicality and wait to see what would happen. I started to feel unsettled going to the other side of my cell block with a large group of South Siders staring at me, including the Albino and Spider Web. For backup. I got Clint, a couple of the Woods, and even some of the Pisas. I grabbed a short #2 pencil, put an eraser on the end of it, and put it between my index and middle finger so that when I punched, it would puncture but stay in my fist. As I had done before, I took off my shirt, went over there, and confronted him in front of everyone.

I said, "You put a hit out on me? Now be a man and finish it. You do it." I was ready to stick that pencil into his throat or his eye and finish the dance from there. The thought of the unknown coming from anybody, anywhere, at any time was scarier than just confronting it head on. He lied and denied it, backing down, and I dissed him in front of his whole crew.

I definitely knew after that, that it was coming. At that point, believe it or not, one of the sheriffs we nick-named "T-Rex," who was one of the meanest sheriffs, pulled me out and said, "Alexsen, you have done the best job we have seen anyone do running a cell block ever. We hate to see you go." I looked at him strangely, and he said, "We just got information that you got a green light and someone's about to kill you." I could swear that they had that cell block bugged. But they were true to their word and they even knew the day I was supposed to get killed, which was in two days. They pulled me out at 4AM that morning and released me early!

The authorities and the police that I had been fighting this whole time had actually saved my life and become my friends. At a later time in my life I would actually start to train with SWAT, help them, and assist the police department in making arrests.

Every month for the next 3 years I had to drive approximately 2 hours in each direction to Santa Ana and check in with my probation officer. He would ask me questions and make sure I was staying in line. If I would have violated my probation in the slightest way, including talking to or having any association (whether on purpose or on accident) with another felon, it was an instant 16 months back to jail.

I remember Clint contacted me once he got released. As much as I wanted to talk to him and thank him, I dared not be in contact with him, lest I violate my probation and go back to jail. And believe me, I could do that on my own. After 3 years, I walked in and my probation officer said, "Congratulations! **98%** of all felons released violate their probation within 3 years and go back to jail." He said, "Good job. You're the top 2%". Wow, for once in my life, I was a top 2% graduate!

You see, the system has a specific was of operating. They get $40,000 a year per inmate, along with $500 per bus ride and $200-400 every time you change from street clothes into jail clothes. It's actually a pretty good racket. Not to mention, the sheriffs are getting overtime. But hey, they need new rims for their muscle cars too, you know.

But seriously, so many guys get busted, clutter our jails, get a tattoo in jail and come out like it's some sort of badge of honor. A lot of them can't function on the outside and actually know how to live in the jail system, and some think it's cool. But it's really not. It's called BEING A CRIMINAL. STOP IT! GROW UP! Get an outside life and take care of your family. They need you. Otherwise, you are just adding to the welfare system and creating more criminals. Being a man doesn't mean you get a woman pregnant, but rather, being a man means accepting responsibility, raising and paying for those kids and working things out in marriage with that woman, as God intended it to be!

CHAPTER 2

SHAKE & BAKE

S OME OF MY BEST YEARS were in my 30s while living in a little house in Sherman Oaks, California. It was around the time of the Rodney King riots and the smoke could be seen, rising from the city. You could smell the tension in the air. Hordes of people were blocking intersections, throwing rocks and bricks through building and car windows and violently pulling people from their vehicles. In addition, the LA Fire Departments being held up with guns for all of their equipment on their fire trucks. Gun shops, sporting goods, and even National Guard armories were broken into and guns were stolen.

Across the street from me was a crazy, Special Forces Vietnam Vet named "Bud". Bud would see the smoke rising from the city of LA, call me over, and we would have a chat. A chat with Bud included him moving a giant china cabinet on wheels, and entering what was a large closet to reveal an arsenal. He would then talk to me about how we were going to deal with looters, rioters, and killers if they came down our block.

I'll omit some of the details to avoid going back to jail, but I will share this much. Bud said, "Andre, you be on roof top with your AK as the sniper; take out the driver to stop the car, and I will pop up out of the bushes and throw my Molotov cocktail (plastic explosive combination that burns 5 times hotter than gasoline and is like Napalm and the broken glass sticks to you) into their car. We used them in Nam. If any of them get out of the car before that, we'll get em! Then we will recon their weapons." At that point, I would repeat his name, "Bud! Bud!! Hey Bud!!!"and snap him out of it, before he went back into the jungle in his mind. But thank God the riots never came to our street. They never knew it was the best thing for them to stay out, because Bud was serious.

At that time, I was living in a remodeled two-bedroom, one bath house off of Ventura Blvd and Van Nuys in Sherman Oaks. It was just me living in that house. I tried the whole roommate thing, but I'm not into the frat house BS and mess and usually prefer to live alone; so I lived with my two Rottweilers. I was working for a cable company at that time. Everyone hated the cable company because they would make you wait all day and their service was shoddy. I was what you called a "subcontractor", so I wasn't an hourly company cable guy, but just there to help.

The other by-the-clock guys were usually the ones out of jail. I had the world's greatest route. Everything south of Ventura Blvd, and everything north of Sunset Blvd from the 405 freeway to the 101 freeway. It was Beverly Hills, Bel Air, Sherman Oaks, Studio City, Hollywood Hills, and Laurel Canyon. Man, the stuff I saw and the people I met you just couldn't believe.

One day I was climbing the telephone poles as I did every day. I usually wouldn't use a climbing rope to hook myself around, but would instead just hold on to one of the other foot pegs or a cable and work with one arm. I know it's kind of crazy, but I did it for years and never fell off; had some close calls though. Was like Vanilla Gorilla. I got offered $200-400 cash per climb up the pole to remove the "traps" that would block out the movie channels. It was a simple system before cable boxes came out. After doing it a few times in one day, I had made $600-800 cash, where the by-the-clock guys would have to wait two weeks for a heavily taxed, small paycheck, hear everyone's complaints and still do side jobs like I did.

I bought a used Toyota white cable truck with ladder racks. It looked like the cable company. I quit the cable company and became the "Robbin Hood of Pirate Cable". The people hated the cable company, and I was their hero. Super rich people in these neighborhoods and their hands were tied with the cable companies. I offered them a solution: Cable Capitalism over cable socialism and monopoly. They loved it.

Next thing you know I was making thousands a week where all my other friends in construction and other fields were breaking their backs and still not making it. I even did better than a lot of studio guys because their work was on and off. I could work any time, seven days a week, and I did. Good times!

At that point I met a guy in Laurel Canyon named Dave. He worked construction. Man, it was like the meeting of Smith and Wesson. We got together and we built an indoor grow room in my garage. Got all the books I could on it, and I had known something about growing marijuana from Hawaii. But this was indoor. It's a science. So, I figured if I could simulate Maui temperatures and trade winds indoors, I'd be rich. And I did.

Not only did I line my rooms with reflect-able Mylar, but I induced Nitrous Oxide, CO_2 that made the plants grow four times faster. I played classical music for the girls- they were all female plants. Male plants have seeds, which you don't want. I was also able to clone cuttings off of one female mother plant and get 60 symmetrical female clones at one time. I used a special orchid cloning gel that nobody else knew about. Everyone else was still on something powdered called "Clonex," and all their clones were dying. Clones are important; you can't restock a room without clones. No clones, no money. I was so good at it that they nicknamed me "Clonan". In addition to the 1000-watt metal halides, Dave learned how to bypass the electrical meter, which was very important. If you don't do that, when the electric guy comes out, we call it "the Frisbee effect". If your meter is spinning like a Frisbee, you're more likely to get busted, and many did.

On top of that, at the end of the cycle, I would leech out my plants, which is to flush all the nutrients and chemicals that makes the pot grow so fast, out with pineapple juice or orange juice. When you smoked it, it actually tasted like pineapple or naval orange. Growers don't do that nowadays. They just juice you with so many chemicals in the marijuana that make you stupid, literally frying your brain. That's why I would never smoke them anymore. I grew up in different times.

By doing all of the things that I did, and simulating the trade winds of Maui, it strengthened the branches to support massive marijuana buds. They were literally the size of coke cans. I have a picture of my hand holding a coke can with my first Rolex from the girls to me, and it was the spear, or thickness, of a coke can.

We were able to pull out $40,000 cash about every two months and things really started rolling then. We were like the *Goodfellas* of the Green World. After the harvest, I would have a bunch of people sit in my front room with plastic on the floor, sponges with rubbing alcohol and scissors and have trimming parties for hours. Rolled Cheech and Chong joints, the thickness of a quarter, and twice as long as a regular cigarette. We were getting stupid. Anyway…

Then I would start on my delivery route. I loved it. I had a black convertible Jeep and would drive around and deliver to celebrity's managers. And sometimes drop off 5 pounds at a time at $5,000 per pound in a silver aluminum Halliburton briefcase. You know, like on *Miami Vice* TV show when they did the big deals. But hey, I thought it's just marijuana, so it's cool. Even the coke dealers would call me and be nice to me to trade me for my bud. And if you know coke dealers, they got an attitude, and you should stay away from them. But they liked the bud.

Things started to get crazy. More and more people started to grow and they needed my help. I took percentages of other grow rooms for my clones, and every generation of clones got stronger in potency than the last. But as greed sets in, so does stupidity. Some of the people that I knew were rock musicians, so we would all go to the Rainbow, where Uncle Mario ran the Roxy, the Whiskey, and the Rainbow. He was the "Godfather of the Sunset Strip" in Hollywood, and I was treated like royalty.

That part of the Sunset Strip was where The Doors got their start. Van Halen played the

Whiskey, and Motley Crue, at their peak, got their start there too. All the craziest bands like

Metallica were all booked by Uncle Mario. Coincidently, I was born and raised in the Hollywood Hills and as a kid in the 60s, I would drive down that Sunset Strip with long hair, a leather fringed vest and leather wrist bands, before Johnny Depp was even born. I was a cool little Hollywood kid who, after my open house school nights in elementary school, would eat ice cream at a little ice-cream shop called C.C. Brown's, next to the Grauman's Chinese Theatre with Jodie Foster, who lived down the block from me. I would always put my feet in John Wayne's foot prints in the cement and hope to be like him one day in films.

Going back to the Rainbow on the Sunset Strip, this was in the days of Guns N' Roses. As you walk through the front door of the Rainbow to the huge front booth facing the fireplace over Axl Rose, was a status symbol. Even the flower girl who sold cocaine in the Rainbow would come and pay her respects; she'd put her bucket down at my table, and when she would leave, there would be a gram of coke in my napkin. And after finishing a round of Pouilly-Fuisse, an expensive bottle of French wine and garlic escargot, the cocaine we called an "after dinner mint".

I would end up upstairs in the exclusive galley of the pirate ship vampire lounge where Mick Jagger and the Rolling Stones, The Who and others would carve their initials into the wood in the booth. It was always after hours, and only VIPs were allowed there. Mario would lock up and we would make long lines on the tables, snorting coke and drinking till the dawn came up. But you could see nothing from the vampire lounge. It was shaped like the under part of the galley of a pirate ship. A true privilege that very rare and few people got to see.

We were all getting into snorting coke too much. The other idiot growers would leave the Rainbow, coked out, and bring people to their house while high and show them their grow rooms. Now, you don't need to be a grower to know how stupid that is! I knew this was the beginning of the end.

If things weren't crazy enough after the riots, I had my grow room set up one house across the street from another and then, wouldn't you know it, the huge 1994 Northridge, California earthquake hits. It had a magnitude 6.7, destroying much of the San Fernando Valley. And right before the earthquake hit, the strangest thing had happened. I kept my money in the banks sometimes, but never really trusted them and still don't. I'm sure some of you can understand why. But right before the earthquake, it was like something or someone, who I now I know was God, had warned me, telling me to remove money from the bank and keep it hidden, and to get blankets, flashlights, and plenty of ammo; I did.

Suddenly, at 4:30AM, my house rocked, and the fireplace peeled away from the wall, causing soot to fall into the room. The vibration was so strong that it managed to unlock my front door and open it. I had fallen asleep on the couch that night, and I don't mind telling you, it freaked me out! The room was filled full of soot and ash and it was such a violent shaking, I thought it was the end of the world. I had been in earthquakes before, but this one was different.

I then began my first Prepper Survival Journey, and I am still on it. I grabbed my two Rottweilers and went outside to assess the damage on the streets. It was a mess. Throughout the block, the pipes had broken on the hot water heaters, the electricity was out and there was smoke coming from some of the houses. I went to Ventura Blvd, a block away, and there were tons of people scared and outside of their houses, all clearly experiencing the aftershock. Whole apartment buildings were caved in and freeways were collapsed and broken.

I went to a Starbucks, and wouldn't you know it, the stupid yuppies in the film industry were standing in front of the Starbucks bragging about the last project they worked on while sipping on free milk from Styrofoam cups. The owner was carting out cases of milk and giving them away because the fridge was broken and there was no electricity. He said, "Take some! Everyone take it!" With one Rottweiler leash on each arm, I squatted down and picked up two big crates of both regular and fat free milk.

I started to carry it off and heard the owner of Starbucks yell "HEY! HEEEEY!!" I turned and thought maybe I took too much, but no, he was yelling at the yuppies, "See that guy? Do what he's doing! Go! Take the milk to your neighbors! What are you sitting around here for?!" I couldn't agree with him more. Unfortunately, I still see plenty of people like that in America. I went down my block to every house, leaving the Rottweilers sitting at the sidewalk guarding the milk as I went up knocking on every door and said, "Fat free or regular?" My neighbors responded, "What are you, a post-apocalyptic milk man?" But they took it and loved it.

Aside from the fireplace that I could board up, the damage to my house extended to the hot water heater. The pipe broke and I thought, "Man, this is going to be a hard fix." Fortunately, my neighbor Stan, so touched by my milk route, said his best friend was a plumber and would be over to fix my hot water heater within a couple of hours.

I remembered that I had hid my money, but hadn't thought to hide food. I went to the market and couldn't believe what I saw. The ceiling had caved in and neither cell phones, nor the ATMs were working. Wow, cash is King! But the markets wouldn't let people in, and I had to figure out where I was going to buy food. Then I kept hearing a voice in my head saying "Vallarta", which was the Mexican food market in Van Nuys. I raced over to find that no none was there. The owner unlocked the door, I grabbed a cart, and I can't tell you how fast I filled it. By the time I reached the door to leave, there was a mob of people trying to get in, all eyeing my cart. I was silently warning, don't even think about it! I could hear the owner in the distance yelling, "NO CREDIT CARDS! NO ATM! CASH ONLY!!" What a trip!

I went home, checked all of my gas for leaks, disconnected the cable and connected it to the antenna on the roof. It was one miracle after another. By night time, all of my neighbors were at my house eating toasted bagels with tea and roasted chicken, watching the news. In the corner of the room was my custom AK-47 with a 55 round nickel-plated magazine, flash lights and blankets. None of the electricity or water at their houses were on for two weeks, but mine was working. I can't exactly explain it, except to say that it was all so unbelievable!

They all ended up leaving for weeks to go to a friend's house until their electricity was back. Except for my house, my whole block was blacked out. It's good to have provisions and be ready, and hear that still small voice. You better listen. I did, and I'm thankful to this day. After the earthquake, I was fed up with that neighborhood and my stupid rock friends, showing everyone their grow rooms. I knew a guy who was an Israeli diamond broker. I can't divulge his name, but he had become a heavy-duty guy from brokering diamonds out of the diamond district in LA and working the money counting rooms in the casinos in Las Vegas. He was connected.

I needed to move fast, and I was in between harvests. I got a hard loan from him with heavy interest, and did what I needed to do. In efforts to get away from people that were starting to go down and get busted, I moved into a house in Coldwater Canyon in Studio City, California. Something told me one night that I needed to stop doing this. I rolled over on a full moon night and saw the moon beam shining off the corner of my nickel-plated magazine on my AK and heard a voice ask, "Are you really going to kill somebody for marijuana plants?" I looked at my Rottweilers, as they were sleeping and protecting me, and I thought, no. So, the clock was ticking.

The house in Coldwater Canyon was private for most part, except I had made a mistake. The landlords lived up the driveway, and I had a grow room in the house. I remember asking the owner of the house a question before I moved in, having heard some rumors about the house from other realtors. I asked "Has anyone been killed in the house? Is it haunted?" I know, strange question.

But there was definitely something wrong in the house that I lived in prior to this one in Sherman Oaks. For a long time, there was an old lady that lived in there, raising her kids. Eventually, she had gotten old and senile and couldn't take care of herself. I remember them telling me that they had to drag the poor old lady out of the house and she was really upset about it. She died shortly after that. But the point is, there was a master bedroom that was hers. That bedroom was always freezing cold and uncomfortable to be in, as if there was a spirit in that room.

So that is why I asked the question at the Coldwater property. The owner looked at me like I was crazy, and said, "Why do you ask that?" I simply replied that I was just wondering. With that, the owner kind of dismissed my question. Anyway, I was close to the Sunset Strip and I could sell my bud to all the clubs and people in Hollywood. I remember thinking, "I gotta get back on set and start doing stunts and acting." The money was good for what I did, but my life had NO purpose!

I remember being so happy when I got cast in a movie called *Wild Bill* with director Walter Hill, who is James Cameron's mentor. James Cameron is my mentor in directing. I worked on a small part on *Wild Bill* at Melody Ranch in Acton California, where John Wayne had shot a lot of his westerns. They recreated the mining town of Deadwood (now South Dakota), where Wild Bill got killed with his infamous "Dead man's hand."

I had such peace and felt great that I was back on set again. I was playing one of the gunmen in Deadwood and I remember there were so many people there. Hundreds of extras on set every morning. It was already 100 degrees out at 7AM. I saw a trailer that everyone was waiting to get into after getting touched up by makeup. They would put dirt on your face, yellow your teeth, and make you look like it was a period piece.

Prior to that, I had stopped by the prop department with some cigars, after hearing the prop guy commenting. He hooked me up with the best rig aka gun belt and Colt 45. It really stood out. Then I remember seeing all the people standing in front of the trailer and said, "Oh hell no, not me." I looked for the trailer for the featured and main actors. It was down the street, and nobody was standing there.

I walked up, and the door opened, and out came Wally Westmore, of the famous Westmore Studio makeup artist. For decades in Hollywood, Michael Wally and his family were the best. He looked at me, saw the gun belt, and said, "Oh, you're one of the gun fighters." I said, "Yes Sir! I sure am." He said, "I'm gonna make you look good." I had a little cigar in the corner of my mouth. I was kind of doing my Clint Eastwood in the *The Good, The Bad and The Ugly*.

He made me squint, and then he put some makeup around my eyes to make the wrinkles stand out. I looked like a main player in the movie, in the desert, squinting. So far, so good. Then all of a sudden, in stepped Jeff Bridges, dressed like Wild Bill Hickok, and he sat right next to me. For the next week, it was just me and Jeff. Why you ask? Because all the other knuckle head actors and extras were down at the end of the street, all crowding around each other, jockeying for a position. Nobody thought to go down to the end of the street to the main actors' makeup trailer. I don't think if I would have asked them if it was Ok, they would have said, "Yeehaw! Go ahead." So, I didn't ask, and I went ahead anyway. And it rocked.

Every morning we would look at the history book of Wild Bill and his Navy Colt Revolvers, taking the time to understand why Wild Bill was so fast and good at what he did. It was just me and Jeff having coffee, getting ready for the scenes. I really got into it. One day, Jeff asked me where I'm from, and since I had lived in Malibu, I told him there; that's where he lived. He proceeded to as ask me, "What are you up to?" I replied, "Trying to get my career going."

I was always standing next to Jeff on set having a cigar, and all the makeup artists would touch both of us up, and spray cans of chilled Evian water on our faces. Meanwhile, all the other schlock's were sweating like French whores. Oops. I think they were playing French saloon girls. The other guys were just too clueless because they were staring at the girls too much to know what was going on. That Friday afternoon, Jeff said to me, "When I walk into the bar, I want you to walk right up to me and say 'Welcome to town, Wild Bill,' like you know me, Ok? I'm giving you a role." I said, "Ok! Awesome!" I was so happy!

One of the A.Ds., who must have drunk some "haterade," was jealous, because every time he had a break to hit on one of the blonde saloon girls, she was too busy showing me attention. All of a sudden, right before the camera was about to roll, the A.D. who had heard what Jeff said to me, grabbed me by the shoulder and said, "If you say that line, you're fired. I swear, I'll make sure." After a warning like that, I didn't know what to do.

I didn't want to be fired, so when the moment came up, I walked up, I mouthed the words, and nothing came out. Stupid. I was gonna wait for another take. Jeff walked over, and asked, "What happened?" I told him what had happened and then he instructed, "Do it again." And I was ready. But then I hear, "That's a wrap everyone! Great shot! We don't need another one." Aww man…I missed my opportunity. I was so bitter and mad that weekend, I couldn't believe it.

I went home, stayed to myself and read the Bible. I said "God, help me if you're real. Straighten this out." Now, I don't see how God could turn back time, so I went in Monday morning as usual, same routine. Looked at the idiot A.D. and he had a smug look on his face. It was at that time I decided to do something I call "trolling," like in fishing. Instead of sitting with all the other extras and actors at lunchtime, I was standing where all the production trailers were. All of a sudden, the production trailer door flew open and it was Walter Hill and Westmore.

Westmore asked Walter as I was walking away, "How about Andre?" and my ears perked up. "Say, what about Andre?" Then they replied, "He'd be perfect!" They knew I did stunts and could ride horses, so I got a better deal. I was now stunt double for lead actor James Remar. I'll never forget sitting in the red stuntman's trailer, own trailer, enjoying the air conditioning while everyone else was outside sweating. Now her I am sitting there reading the Bible and smoking a cigar with a totally different look, from a gun fighter extra, and now to the James Remar character stuntman, who was a killer and gun fighter. I looked out as the A.D. walked past the window of my trailer. I made a gesture at him, pointing to him laughing my ass off. And there was not a darn thing he could do about it. Go drink some more haterade, 'cause you're now trying to be in my Kool-Aid, and don't even know the flavor!

God had given me the upgrade, and the fun part to do. It was even better than what I could have done before. Later, I would perfect what I call "the art of the upgrade" on movie sets. It would lead me to and through my great present-day credits and career.

One day, my landlord asked me what I did for work and why I could be home so often. I said I worked in entertainment as a stuntman/actor and we don't always work regular hours. They must have suspected something, because they told me that a real estate broker was coming to the house for an appraisal and needed to look all around. Hmmm...what to do?

I had my cousin come over with his girlfriend since I couldn't dismantle the whole grow room. It was in the house rather than in the garage. I came up with a story that I'd be at work and that they would be there to let the broker and to make sure that the Rottweilers were Ok. Anyway, my cousin knew what was going on and his girlfriend concocted some sort of awful stew in a pot on the stove that stunk on purpose, because the grow room smelled like skunk, which is high grade marijuana. I was nervous for days before and after. I locked the bedroom door with a deadbolt lock and told the broker, my cousin and the owners of the house that it was my office, and I forgot to leave the key. Stupid, but it worked.

After that, I was very uneasy living at that house, and people had been starting to look for me where I use to live. At the time, I was in such a hurry that I had changed my number and just moved. I guess it freaked people out. One night I found myself distraught, depressed and not knowing what to do. I was starting to hit bottom. I had had a couple of drinks, and I remember going into the master bedroom, and almost in a daze, grabbing my AK47, chambering it, and leaning on it with my heart and my hand on the trigger. Thank God my best friend was there at the time and he happened to walk in the room. "What are you doing?!!" I remember looking up at him in a daze and I said, "Wow. I don't know." I had almost killed myself. I had a best friend, who had tragically shot himself in the heart years before that. So that whole scenario freaked me out!

Some time later, in that same bedroom, I was sound asleep with a girl I was dating at the time. Simultaneously, we suddenly woke up out of a dead sleep. I turned on the light immediately. We looked at each other wide eyed, and at the same time said, "Do you feel that?!" It was cold in the room and there was an overwhelming evil presence. I can't explain it, but it would have been really scary to anybody. I remember having a Bible there that my best friend left. The only thing I knew to do was to read it out loud. I remember reading the Bible, and whatever it was, left, and then there was peace. Later in my life, I found out why.

I recall being upset and talking to the owner of the house, asking her once again "What happened in this house?!" What she said gave me chills.

"A young man committed suicide in the master bedroom (where I almost did, and where that spirit was felt) …and other people who lived there reported objects flying around the room, and a telephone flying out the front door, and a jewelry box being thrown out the door…with nobody standing there. I thought the people who said that must have just been high." They were not high. Something was really wrong there. And that demonic spirit wanted me to join the other guy who killed himself. That was it for me. I was done, and had to get out of LA.

CHAPTER 3

LIFE'S ROLL OF THE DICE

I HAD TO FIND ANOTHER WAY to make money since I had gotten used to having a lot. I liquidated everything I had, dismantled my grow rooms, sold all my gear and got rid of my AK and my slant nose 911 Porsche. I met an old man who taught me to play the system of 21 black jack. And I thought, Vegas! I'll go hide out, play cards, stay to myself, do personal security and get lost in the crowd. It wasn't a big winning system, with an average of $300 an hour; and you don't drink alcohol when you do it. You drink coffee and you keep your wits about you because they like to throw in dealers in Vegas who do cheat and try to take your bank. I had been asked to leave a couple of casinos.

I also went to work as a VIP bodyguard for executives and their families. And with that too, you can't drink until you are done working. Sometimes I would go out with the locals and our night out would start around 7AM till about noon. At first, I thought I had it made. You could drink alcohol for free there. During the week, the town is mostly locals but its 4 to 1...women to men. There were casino girls, show girls, dancers, strippers and porn stars, and with the buffet and the comps, you could eat like a King. And after all of that, the mellowest family restaurant was Hooters. Strange huh?

It took a while, but it became depressing and deflating, witnessing people in the casinos, day in and day out, losing their money, their hopes and their dreams. My schedule would consist of sleeping till about 4 or 5PM, going to Golds Gym to tan and train, and some days I would go to Vegas Aikido. There was a guy named Sensei Gregory who would talk about the Lord. Some of it sunk in, but I didn't get all of it until later. It wasn't long until I was getting known around Vegas. Believe it or not, it's a small town and you run into a lot of the same people.

Before going to bed at dawn, many nights I would go into the Mirage and say good night to my friends. The only ones I could relate to, because I felt the same as they did…trapped. They were the magnificent white Bengal Tigers. I would stare at them, and they would look back. I could tell each one apart because I would stare at them for so long, saying, "One day, I'm going to be training and rescuing Tigers." I didn't know how it would come into fruition, but I had a dream.

An incident had occurred that led me to believe that I had pretty much bottomed out. I was drinking in a bar about 7AM with the locals. I saw a nicely dressed, drunk guy in the corner getting pushed around by a couple of rough looking guys. So, I went over there and bailed him out. The other guys could see that I wasn't the one, so they didn't mess with me. I shook his hand like I knew him and pulled him out of the corner. Good thing too for him. He took a minute and decorated his shoes, if you know what I mean, and I just knew I couldn't leave him alone in that condition. I asked him if he had a car, thinking I could put him in it so he could go to sleep. He gave me the keys pointed outside to a stretch limo.

Before he passed out for a few hours, he said I could do what I wanted, and that if I wanted to drive it, I could. This is where the plot gets a bit movie-like. On the seat, I noticed a cell phone and a pager going off. I had a few rum and cokes in me, so I picked up the phone and dialed back the pagers. I would ask, "Who dis?", and they would ask me "Where are you?", and I'd say, "I'm coming to pick you up." I would drive to pick them up, and it turned out to be a couple of working girls with some customers.

They poured into the back and started drinking. I kept drinking too, driving all over town. We made stops, picked up more people, dropped people off, picked up drugs and dropped off drugs. I was having a pretty good time. Through all of the noise, the limo driver was still passed out in the back. I just told everyone I was the replacement driver.

There was one particular guy that was really drunk and a serious smart ass. I was sarcastic too, so it was funny, for a bit. Anyway, we pulled into the back parking area of some condos into the and were kind of in between the rows of the garages and the condo. One of the people in my limo ran in to get something. Suddenly, what seemed like all of Clark County Sheriff's department and S.W.A.T. in Las Vegas blocked me in on all sides. The big S.W.A.T. truck was parked behind the limo, and agents started to get out with all kinds of weapons, from shotguns to ARs to hand guns, battering rams, shields, helmets, you name it. And I thought, "Oh shit. I've done it this time. They have tracked me down from LA." I thought that was it!

Instead, they started to run past the limo in formation repeating "Hut, hut, hut, hut, hut..." and stormed the condo and the building screaming through megaphones, "GET ON THE GROUND!" Above came the helicopters, yet nobody messed with the limo. I couldn't believe it. Here I was in this limo with all these people, surrounded by drugs and alcohol. I just pulled the keys out of the ignition, as if to say I wasn't driving, poured another drink, and enjoyed the drive-in movie in front of me. It was seriously unreal. They were pulling people out of there in hand cuffs, criminals, girls, drug dealers, and I don't know who and what else!

The idiots in the back are trying to tell me "Get us out of here." I said "What do I look like? I dream a Genie? You want me to nod my head and make us disappear? Turn around you idiots. That giant grill behind you, that looks like an armored car, is a S.W.A.T. vehicle and they are hard to drive over." So, we all had to wait, which was fine with me, but these people were starting to piss me off. Once it was over and I was back on the road driving, the smart ass started to give me a hard time.

I told him, "Don't make me come back there." He said, "I wish you would." Right then, as I was turned around, not paying attention, the light turned red and I punched it, turning the limo sideways. I guess you refer to it as drifting nowadays, but that was my stunt driving background. I had everyone to one side of the limo on top of each other, spilling drinks on the smart ass. But wouldn't you know it? The only motorcycle cop around was watching me and started to chase us.

Alcohol was spilt all over the place, and I wreaked of it. I had just run a red light, pitching a stretch limo sideways, and God only knows what various drugs were in the car. So, I thought to myself as Bugs Bunny would say in his cartoons, "Think fast, rabbit!" I pulled over the limo real fast, ran to the back of it, opened the door, and it was perfect. The smart ass got out first and I started to yell at him in front of the cop, "YOU GUYS ARE ALL OUT OF CONTROL! YOU GOTTA GET OUT OF THE LIMO NOW!" I turned to the cop and said, "Thank God you pulled me over officer! I was gonna call for backup and assistance!" Then I calmed down and let the smart ass do the rest. He was spitting, slurring and drunk. The girls were pouring out of there, and the cop had his hands full. I said, "Officer, I have a very important VIP client to pick up. You got this from here?" He let me go. I left the gang of gaggles on the corner with the cop.

After all that, I mixed another drink and rolled to my next call. I picked up a couple more working girls and took them where they needed to go. Then, all of a sudden, I heard the limo driver wake up and start screaming, "You stole my $100!" as one of the girls was walking off. I knew she did it. I chased her down, and I said, "I'm sober. And I know what's going on. And I could call for Las Vegas P.D. in a second and have you arrested. They know me. Now you give me that $100." She lied the first time, claiming she didn't take it. Then I told her I saw her do it and she bowed her head, pulling the crumpled $100 back out. I gave it back to the limo driver and he was starting to kind of wake up.

By the end of it all, I was spent. It was about 1pm and it was hot out. The part was over and I needed to go get some sleep. Nobody rides for free in my limo, so I had made some money, and it was kind of fun. At that point, I had done almost all you can do in Vegas. And then, the unthinkable happened. I was in Vegas to get away from everyone in LA, and that included the Israeli mobster and diamond broker who I owed hard loan money.

Wouldn't you know it? I'm in the Plaza Casino and I back up to a door. Apparently, it was to the money counting room. The door opens and it's the Israeli mob leader with a bag of money. His hand on my shoulder, so I said, "Hey! What are you doing here? I was just about to call you!" We had a serious talk and he said that whatever was about to happen to me was now out of his control.

Uh-oh! that's what they say when somebody else is going to do something horrible to you. They try to cover it up by saying, "It's out of my hands." Fortunately, we were able to work it out by me doing some work for them, running higher end working girls to high end hotel rooms and making sure they came back, with the money. So, while it wasn't the way I expected to work off what I owed, I guess I did my VIP bodyguard work.

At that point, I started to feel an overwhelming sense that everything was wrong and there was a lot of evil around me. I was living like a vampire and I couldn't take it. I was losing my mind. Desperate, I picked up a Bible in the hotel and started to read it. It had worked for me before when I felt evil around me. I felt especially comforted when I read the red letters, which stood for the words of Jesus himself. I would try going for a drive into the hills to find grass and trees that were natural. I even went to Lake Pyramid, wrote all of my problems on a piece of paper, and threw it into the lake, praying for God to take them. I had nowhere else to run. Not to mention, everyone in LA had gotten busted, one grow room after another. And here I was, gone. So, what do you think they thought? Yup, me; but it wasn't. I had just gotten out because I heard that "still, small voice".

Something amazing then happened to me. The Israeli mob leader wanted to talk to me. He told me that his 5-year-old little boy, who was his pride and joy, had developed a serious brain tumor. Now this guy would go to temple, he would pray and he would read the Torah, which is the first ten books of the Bible. Almost crying, he said to me, "I couldn't help but feel that God is punishing me for all the people that I hurt. And I don't mean their feelings." He then looked at me, and told me to go. With his Israeli accent, he further implored, "Go, my friend, and don't look back. Nobody will be there, nobody will come after you or hurt you." He released me and any hold on my life. Now, people like that don't just let you walk out when you know as much as I knew. So, between that and the Bible, the only thing that gave me peace, it was over. I had had enough, and it was time for me to leave Las Vegas…Sin City.

The last thing I saw before I left was Motley Crue's guitarist and Nikki Sixx's Harley Davidson on display at the Hard Rock Café. On a brass plaque on his gas tank, it read, "…Forward my mail to me in Hell…" And that's where I felt I was headed if I didn't get out of there. Eventually, once in a better state of mind, I would see Nikki Sixx again. He lived near me and I did some bodyguard work for Vince Neil and Motley Crue.

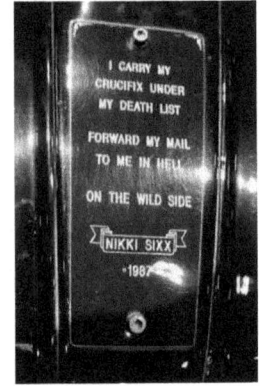

In a car that somebody else had rented me, I packed up all I had. By sunset, I was driving over the hill and leaving Las Vegas, never to look back! I felt peace. I didn't know where I was going or what I was going to do, but I knew that what I was doing wasn't working. The definition of insanity is doing the same thing over and over and expecting different results. Plus, I always knew that I was destined to do something great and grand. So, I wanted to turn over my life. How, I didn't know, but I would soon find out.

CHAPTER 4

AMERICA'S MOST WANTED

I HEADED BACK TO LA. All the great money I was making while doing the wrong things was a big distraction and a waste of my time. I always knew for years, working on and off in the industry, that what I really wanted to do, and what I was destined for, was to work on TV and feature films.

Upon coming into LA, I didn't know how I was going make the amounts of money I used to, but I had peace about it. I signed up with some casting agencies and told people I was back in the loop. I got a little role in a movie called *Multiplicity* with Michael Keaton. Boy, was he a jerk, and I always call it like I see it. He went from Mr. Mom to Mr. PMS.

I met two brunettes that were very attractive. After coming from Vegas, where good men are a valued commodity for women being that its 4-1, I thought I'd be a hot shot and ask them both out until I decided which one I wanted. They said, "Let's go hang out Sunday, all of us!" and I thought Ok, freaky! They instructed to meet them around 11AM in Studio City. It actually ended up being the address of a church called "In His Presence Church," run by a Pastor Mel and his wife, Pastor Desiree. At first, I was a bit thrown off that we were at a church. But then the girls asked "Is there something wrong? Are you coming in?" as if to say, "You're not scared, are you?"

Now mind you, I had come from the religious background of Greek Orthodox. My knowledge of church was seeing a priest in an all-black gown, with a giant long grey beard and some sort of a squared off black hat, swinging incense on a chain and chanting in Latin. At some point, I remember asking if I was I going to Heaven; the answer was yes. When I asked why, they said, "You were dedicated as a child, and were baby baptized". That means the priest squirted you with some holy water and I'm sure a couple of Latin chants came out of his mouth. Bada Bing! I was thinking I was in the club, going to Heaven! Not so. I had religion, but not a relationship with the Lord, and that's the most important part about Christianity. Christian means Christ follower, and I was far from that. I had missed the mark. And that's what the word sin means: to miss the mark, like an archer does.

I came to find out that Pastor Mel had a lot in common with me. He was a former cocaine addict and alcoholic who had given his life over to God one morning, sitting in traffic on the freeway after dropping his friends off from a night of partying. He had reached bottom, and so had I. Desiree, his wife, was an actress/stuntwoman that got so badly burned by a stunt gone wrong that it was amazing she was even alive. So, I had something in common with her too, being a stuntman.

The whole church was great and very different from Greek Orthodox. This Spirit-filled, bible-believing, non-denominational Christian church was full of ex-drug addicts, alcoholics, crackheads and people in the industry that were sick and tired of being sick and tired. This was right where I needed to be, and for the first time in my life, I knew it. When the alter call came up to receive Jesus and a relationship, not a religion, I lost it. I raised my hand, walked up to the altar and received the Lord. Best thing I had ever done in my life. God had a different idea and plan for me than what I initially thought was going to be something cool and casual with these two girls. From that day on, I looked at those two girls like they were my sisters, rather than prey to stock. I looked at all women differently. My dad had been a womanizer, alcoholic and more. I wanted to be the complete opposite, so I set out to fulfill my mission!

A couple of days later, I had bought a huge silver cross to represent my huge faith. I recall being stuck in traffic on Sunset Strip, driving in a hot car with no air conditioning and looking up at a giant billboard of a rapper named Tupac Shakur. I remember cursing him, even being racist and calling him the N word, wondering why the heck this guy was making money while I'm stuck in this car.

That night I got a phone call from a casting director. She asked if I did stunts and worked with weapons; I said yes. She said, "I need you to play an L.A.P.D. sergeant tomorrow for some music video." I was broke, to be honest with you, so I showed up the next morning. And guess who the star of the music video was! God had a humbling surprise for me. It was Tupac Shakur, along with Snoop Dogg, Nate Dogg, Warren G, Geodesy and Suge Knight of Death Row Records.

I gotta tell you, I was blown away. I needed to get a camera, but I was broke. I reached inside the sergeant's uniform that they had put me in to find that there was $40 cash in there. I asked the wardrobe lady, "Was this somebody else's costume before me?" She said, "No. It's yours. Why, does it not fit well?" To which I replied, "Everything is perfect, Ma'am."

I ran from the night club, known as "The Gate" on La Cienega Blvd, to the liquor store next door and grabbed a disposable camera, and then had to wait for the gate to be unlocked when I returned. You see, Tupac had just survived being shot 5 times at close range in New York City after coming out of a recording studio. It was suspected to be a hit by the rapper Biggie Smalls, to which I digress. The gates and barbed wire fencing a means of protection against the infamous East Coast/West Coast rap war that was initiated. Now you may find this is silly, but it was of the utmost seriousness to all the Crips, Bloods, and the other 20 guys on Tupac's set, strapped and armed to the teeth, including two of the most solid built guys, carrying MAC-10s. It was all too real.

And here I was, dressed like a L.A.P.D. sergeant. To them, even though I was an actor, I looked and played the part, complete with all the props, including handcuffs, gun, radio and sergeant stripes. They had been arrested so many times that it was just subliminal to look at me and think I was real. Aside from the seriousness of the scenario, it was kind of funny being on set because Pac's would have cases of Louis Roederer Cristal Champagne, Alize and Hennessy delivered from the liquor store next door. If that wasn't enough, huge marijuana joints were flowing all day.

It seemed like every time I would come around a corner, someone would be rolling a philly blunt, aka fat joint. They would just say "Drey! You gotsta stop creeping around the corner like that." I was just walking around the set, but it wasn't me, it was them I think. By morning, cameras were rolling to film the first take of "2 of Amerikaz Most Wanted (Ain't Nothin' but a Gangsta Party." They told me to kick in the door of the night club, come in with S.W.A.T., grab Pac, put a gun to him and drag him outside. I was feeling pensive and uneasy about that, so Tupac pulled me aside and said, "Drey, are you not an actor? I know I hired the right guy. Dude, play the role. Don't worry about hurtin' me."

At that moment, I recall having learning method and emotional acting from Howard Fine Acting Studio. Draw back into your mind a certain moment in time and recreate it in your head. Be in that moment, and when you become interested, you become interesting. I replied Ok to Pac and took a minute to compose myself. I thought about the Rodney King riots, thought about the anger at the billboard shot and thought about what I was really here to do.

Take 2. I stormed the club, grabbed Pac, put a model 1911 Colt 45 to his head and yanked his ass out of the booth. I could almost swear that he caught some air. I threw him out of the club, holding him by the back of the shirt. I realized when the cameras stopped, that maybe I went a little overboard. Everything was silent and everyone was staring at me. I was feeling a small sense of anxiety until Tupac clapped his hands together, started laughing and said, "YEAH! Get this motherfucker an agent!" We didn't need another take.

The next day I was supposed to work with Calvin Broadus from LBC, Long Beach City, aka

Snoop Dogg. He was standing quiet, tall in a 30s style gangster suit with a fedora. I said, "I wanna meet the man before I work with him." They said, "Drey, now ain't a good time. Don't go messin' with him." I asked what's wrong. They said, "His pit-bull jumped off the balcony in Malibu and hung itself last night." That was even part of the lyrics in the song.

I got quiet for a moment, then proceeded to walk towards him. Everyone said, "Oh shit," and tried grabbing me by the shirt. I approached him and started to talk to him. Everyone watched as Snoop had his head down and was staring at me right in the eyes. Then his eyes got teary and he shook my hand and gave me a half hug.

I walked back towards everyone and they said, "Are you crazy? What'd you say to him?" I said the only thing I could say to a man in that situation, that I had been there. My favorite purple-ribbon winning pit-bull, Bruzer, had jumped out my horse stable, which he was chained to inside, and hung himself out the window. And I found him there that way. Long before Snoop Dogg was Snoop Dogg, I had pit-bulls. It was something he related to, and all was cool.

A bright pink metallic 500 SL Mercedes pulled up and out climbed a giant African American guy in all bright-pink silk pants and a pink silk top, with more jewelry than Tiffany's. I asked, "Who that in the PJs?" They said, "Drey, ya shouldn't be sayin' that. That's Suge Knight. He's a killa and he owns Death Row Records." I kind of nodded my head and said, "He cool."

This is when all the shit started to get crazy. I had worked a couple more music videos for Pac back-to-back. He had given me great money, a great trailer on set to stay in and even offered me some of what he called a "gang of hos." But I was all right. He had treated me better than most people I had known for years, and since he didn't want to keep hiring new people because of the near-death stuff, familiarity was important to him, and we became friends. He taught me quite a few things. To me, Pac was more of a poet than a rapper, and there will never be anybody in the rap game or a lyrical poet greater than my friend, Tupac Shakur.

I had some great times working on "How Do You Want It" and "All About You" right after "2 of Amerkaz Most Wanted". In "How Do You Want It," he attempted to do a version for *Playboy*. We showed up in the morning to a Victorian themed western bar scene with girls we had never seen before; he had hired real female porn stars. In the words of the guys on set, "Dez bitches be dropping E by 11AM and high as a mofo by noon." We rolled first take, and clearly, these girls were comfortable with gyrating and ripping off their clothes. Even though we are men with healthy appetites for beautiful, we were kind of like "Wow, way over the top. What are we filming here?" I even found out one of them dosed my orange juice in the limo without me knowing it. Wasn't funny.

So again, Pac being the man he is, yelled out, "CUT! CUT! CUT!" He pulled all the men to the corner of the bar, and said to all of us, "Y'all don't understand. I'm tryin' to throw a party for y'all here, and I brought these girls in for you. And all you guys do is kinda stand around like some kind of manikins?" He ordered his A.D. to bring all of us a tray of Hennessy shots, while he proceeded to roll another blunt. He insisted we do a couple of shots, smoke a joint with him, and then yelled for playback, and the cameras rolled. By then, we were motivated and comfortable. Too much. After all that, the footage was unusable, even for *Playboy*, because it was too racy.

I'll never forget the time Pac went to lunch one day and came back an hour late. He apologized to everyone but had come back with two brand new, just bought vehicles, a black Humvee and a black Bentley convertible. He christened the Bentley by popping open the glove compartment and rolling a huge blunt telling everyone, "don't stand away from the car, don't trip, it's for all of us to enjoy." He put on some of his music in the Bentley and we all partook in the christening. He eventually gave both cars to two important friends of his.

Before he did that, coming through the gate were a couple of vultures. There were all kinds of rappers trying to get in on the set and in the music video. This particular rapper was previously famous, but managed to blow through $59 million, and was now broke. You all know him as M.C. Hammer. Well, he crowded around Tupac's Bentley at the gate and said, "Pac, my man. Hook a nigga up and put me in your video." Pac looked at Hammer and said, "Where were you to hook a nigga up when I was running pagers in Oak Town and breaking away from Digital Underground?" then proceeded to run over M.C. Hammer's feet with his Bentley as the gate got slammed in his face, shutting him out and his sorry ass entourage. That's what I call "Hammer Time."

It seemed to humor Pac and his gangster friends if they could get a picture with me. I asked, "...with ME?" and they said, "Yeah! Lemme see your gun." I said Ok. They would put it to my head and ask me to make a serious look, all the while, I'm dressed like LAPD. I made good at making scary police faces and humoring them. Because you never know, and they had my back too. Someone might look through the gate, see me as a cop and want to blast a fool!

I have played more cop roles than anyone in Hollywood, and was even the cop in the California Highway Patrol's campaign, "Click it or ticket" for a couple of years. I got really good at it, and later in life, even got temporary badges for making arrests undercover for L.A.P.D. Boy. But that's a story for later.

There were also real LAPD that showed up on set every now and then. It was funny because a couple of them actually mistook me for a sergeant. So, I let it be. I even ran interference for some of them if they were rolling something. I'd call out, "It's 5.0," aka popo, one-time, da man or the police. It was Friday afternoon and we had just wrapped up "All About You." Tupac had just gotten done making us all his famous chicken wings. He kept a little fryer in his car with him. I can't explain it. A cultural thing, maybe. But it was awesome.

He was about to leave for Las Vegas and he and I were standing in the kitchen, talking about my cross. I started to talk to him about God, and I wished I would have talked more. That was the last time I would ever see my friend Pac. He got shot that night in Las Vegas, Nevada, and died the following week. I had learned a lot, and hope to see him on the other side. There were two people that talked to him about God before he died; it was me, and Evander Holyfield. It was almost as if he knew his time was soon coming to its end. Tupac said, "I wonder what will happen after this..." He asked me, "Does that cross make you feel closer to God?" I just told him it reminds me that God is always near and close by, and that it also reminds me of where I'm headed, to Heaven, because I have Jesus!

CHAPTER 5

HIGHWAY TO HELL

AFTER THE DEATH OF TUPAC, I felt I needed to get away from town and do something outside of LA. I wound up meeting a night club owner of a huge bar in Ventura County. I got involved in running the club and becoming a business partner. More and more, I was starting to realize that something was wrong with my Christian walk. Getting back to joints, nightclubs, and drinking. It wasn't good.

I walked into a hardware store in Camarillo, wearing my silver cross, when I was approached by a guy named Paul, who wore a big wooden cross around his neck with an eye hook and leather strap. He asked me about my cross, saying, "Nice cross. Is it for decoration?" I told him it wasn't. He asked, "What does it mean to you?" I replied, "It's a reminder of my Lord and Savior Jesus and what He did for me on the cross." He seemed satisfied with that answer and gave me his phone number, saying, "You met me for a reason. I'm supposed to teach you to be a Warrior for God, a spiritual and prayer warrior." I kind of shrugged my shoulders, took his phone number, and thought to myself "Ok weird guy named Paul, with the big wooden cross."

It was shortly after that, that I had seen a special on TV regarding people's head injuries, and what to do in the event of an emergency. That same day, I was giving lessons to a girl I was seeing on how to drive my Mustang. It was a convertible CHP version, one of the first Mustangs that the highway patrol incorporated into their high-speed chases. These cars were so fast and light; it was the only thing they could use to catch other Mustangs and fast cars. I don't know why I was showing her this, but I was teaching her how to drive this stick shift car in the event of a slide in any case.

I noticed that she was driving the car with the seatbelt under her arm. Since this car was a convertible, I asked her if she would please put the seatbelt over her shoulder. She said it wrinkled her dress, but Ok. After her brief stunt driving course, I dropped her off. On the way home, a still, small voice had urged me to get the thickest leather strap I could find for my cross. So, I bought one and put it on that night.

The next day, I was leaving my house in the San Fernando Valley to go out to Santa Barbara with my girl for the day. Right before I left my house, and for the first time, I actually heard God speak to me audibly. He told me to stay and pray with him longer. This kind of surprised me, but I listened. I knelt at the steps near the front door, where I never pray. I don't remember what I prayed for exactly, however, I listened to God's instruction.

I picked her up, and she wanted to drive. I said Ok, and off we went onto the 101 freeway, towards Oxnard, with the convertible top down. It was July 27th at 1:30 in the afternoon on a stretch of highway known as "blood alley." Many deaths that occurred there due to a high-speed embankment and lanes angled incorrectly, which stacked and pushed all the cars and made them drift towards the fast lane. It was there that a car was coming over to our lane at almost 70 mph, and I thought for sure it was going to stop. But it didn't. It hit the front end of my small Mustang and put my car into a slide.

From this point on, everything started to happen in slow motion. The car slid until the rear tires caught the pavement and the posi-traction rear end kicked in, shooting the car at an angle toward the wall, and vaulting us into the air like some sort of a Hollywood movie stunt. Unfortunately, this was no stunt. There was no roof or roll bar, and this car was small, light and shallow, unlike the bigger Mustangs of today.

We started to tumble on the highway and landed upside down. The windshield, and what held it in place, had collapsed, and the high back seats from the highway were sheared down a good foot. So, what happened to my head? When we shot at the wall and hit it, my thick leather strap got caught on one of the only emergency hand breaks in a car on the passenger side, keeping my head down during the whole tumble and high-speed roll. It was a one in a million miracle, and it was done by God!

When the car stopped rolling, it landed upside down and I was choking on something. I didn't realize what was going on at that moment, but it was the leather strap. Once I unhooked it, I could feel the hot asphalt from the highway within inches of my face and the side of my head. Since the windshields had collapsed, and the seats were sheared off, it was dark, like I was in a boat upside down. The noise was deafening. I flailed to get out of the car and crawled out of the wreckage, in view of both rear tires at chest level screaming and smoking. The car was still in gear!

I wasted no time getting to her side of the car, thinking she was dead for sure. As I got to her side, I saw a huge pool of blood collecting and I wretched on the door until it opened. She was fading in and out of consciousness as I pulled out her limp body. The top of her head was mangled. Remembering what I saw on the EMT episode, I took off my shirt, elevated her legs and pressed down on her head. Her wrist had a compound fracture and was severely bleeding as well. When the car landed upside down, the windshield collapsed onto the steering wheel, pinning her wrist to the highway and grinding it into the asphalt.

I saw my crushed cell phone and got one phone call off to 911. I could barely hear them and wasn't even sure if I got through. But no matter, the wreck was so big, it shut down the whole freeway. I then looked up into the sun in a daze...it was surreal. A short time after, I felt a rubber hand on my shoulder. "I'm an off-duty paramedic. I was right behind you. I've got this." Miracle after miracle was happening. And here I was in white shorts, and not a scratch on me.

If I had been the one driving on that highway, my head wouldn't have had anywhere to go and would have been ground down like hamburger meat down to my chest. She was a good foot shorter than me. The ambulance arrived and started to put her on a gurney. As they were loading her onto the ambulance, one of the EMTs said I couldn't go. I went at him to grab him by his lapels and shook the shit out of him. The other ambulance driver calmed us down and urged, "Let him go. He can help." So, she was laying on the gurney, supine, and they placed me behind her, with her head between my legs. My job was to keep her awake. The TV special informed that losing consciousness with a head injury could cause you to either die or go into a coma. The EMT instructed, "Talk to her. Keep her awake and tell her whatever you need to say." And I did.

We got to the hospital. They ran her in STAT for brain trauma surgery and there were nurses running all over the place. They called in trauma surgeons and specialists for traumatic brain injury operations. One of the main on-call nurses came running in and said, "My God! I saw the car. How many are dead this time!?" A nurse pointed to me and said, "Ask him". I was standing there with an illuminating light coming through the two open hospital doors between my arms and my legs. It was rays of white light. It was very angelic. The nurse asked if I had seen the accident. I said, "No, I was in the car." She was a very polite and proper looking lady. She said, "No fucking way you were in that car!!! Last week 4 people all died at that same place in a roll in a Ford hardtop 4 door LTD." I explained to her that it was my cross that saved me from being ejected and dying. She said, "Don't ever take that cross off." I replied, "It's not the cross. It's the meaning behind it."

While she was in the OR, I was praying that she would be alright. At that point, my sister showed up at the hospital, white as a ghost. She had seen the wreckage of what was left of the car on the highway with all the blood. She couldn't believe that I was standing in front of her without a scratch. I have wrecked cars on purpose for TV and films, but never in my wildest dreams could I imagine doing it without a roll bar, safety harness and helmet. As for the chowder head that cut me off, thanks a lot for leaving us for dead and taking off, not even checking to see if we were alive. We were told later that there was a phone call to the police department of a very concerned man wondering if we were okay. WE'RE FINE! THANKS A LOT FOR ASKING!

A group of people came to the hospital that I either knew from the club, or encountered at the time of the accident. People had pulled over on the side of the freeway and jumped the fence to help me, but I was too dazed at the time to reply. As for the girl, the operation was successful, and she pulled through just fine. Right after that, I started tripping out in my head. What was this all about? I couldn't believe it. Hearing God's voice, the leather strap, the stunt-driving course, the EMT special that I watched…it was a miracle that I survived. At that point, something hit me, and I decided to call Paul, the weird guy with the wooden cross.

When I called him, I told him what had happened. He was as calm as could be, like, no big deal. And then he totally blew my mind. Here's the truth that he imparted, "You have spent years dealing and selling drugs, making a dishonest living and whether you believe it or not, you were helping the enemy, Satan. But now that you have given your life over to Jesus, you're no good to him. He wants you dead. You got a target on your back." It started to make sense. I asked him what I was supposed to do. He said, "Learn how to fight better." I asked him how. He said, "I told you. God put me in your life to prepare you for spiritual warfare, and to be in His army and be a prayer warrior. Satan's job is to rob, kill and destroy, and his greatest trick is making people believe he doesn't exist and that he will actually give things to those working for him to pacify them so they will not need or believe in God. But at the end of your life, when you wake up after your first death on earth and you're in the presence of

God, judged and separated, you could end up in Hell, which was set up for Satan and the demons." WOW!

He continued and gave me some peace. "Do not be afraid. Jesus conquered the enemy, death and the grave, so you have authority over Satan, in Jesus name. Jesus preached about the Kingdom of God. He healed the sick, raised the dead, taught people to repent of their sins and casted out demons. Demons were fallen angels created by God. And Jesus is the Son of God. The demons know who He is and are afraid of Jesus. And since you received Jesus, you are a child of God, and you have authority over them, in Jesus name."

Heavy duty stuff. But as I came to find out, everything Paul said was true. There's a physical world that we live in, and a spiritual world that we don't see. But it's very real. And if you can learn to do battle in the spiritual world, in Jesus name and by His authority, you will be okay in the physical world. So, I embarked into the Spiritual Gladiator World. And wow, what I started to see in both worlds, nothing could have prepared me for. And any movies they make on this…NOTHING compares to the real thing. We will talk about this later.

After the phone conversation, I prayed to God to go to work for Him. I said, "God, I am not afraid of blood, car wrecks and carnage. I can deal with it. Use me to help others in similar situations." And man, I tell you, you better be careful what you pray for, because I got it!

One day, I was working out at the gym and there were two EMTs there. I was showing them how I do shoulder exercises, and I could hear that they had their radios on. Normally I drive to the gym, but I had walked that day. As I was going back home from the gym, a speeding minivan almost clipped me and rounded the corner way too fast. I heard a horrific wreck, so I ran around the corner, where I saw the minivan completely rolled over on its side after hitting a Mercedes.

I ran over, and I still don't quite remember how I got up there, but I had jumped up on top of that van so fast and was looking through the passenger side glass window at the driver from above, it was a little Asian lady. At that point I tried to open the passenger side door standing on top, but couldn't. She had pinched the door jamb by side sweeping the Mercedes, and the door wouldn't open.

I then realized that the rear tire was still spinning, and the van started smoking. At that point, I was even more motivated, and I gave it all I had. I kid you not, I heard sheet metal bending, as I wretched the door open. Adrenaline is a powerful thing. I reached down, grabbed her by the wrist, and snatched her up like she was a Pekingese Chihuahua!

Then I put her on the top of the van, jumped down and swept her off the van to safety. I had come to realize that she was concerned about a cell phone that left in the car. It on the driver's side in the corner of the windshield. I'm thinking, what's the deal with the cell phone? Then I realized she was on the phone when she hit the Mercedes. At that point I felt like the phone Nazi. And said, with my best Asian accent, "No mo cell phone fo you!"

A crowd had started to gather. As I was heading back home, the two EMTs from the gym arrived. At that point, a neighbor on the lawn was explaining to everybody what had happened. He said, "...and this guy leaped on top of the van and pulled this woman out so easily to safety. It was amazing!" The two EMTs looked at the neighbor and asked who. "Who did this?" He pointed to me and said, "That's the guy!!" One of the EMTs said in his Brooklyn, NY accent, "You? Who are you, frickin' supaman?" I kind of laughed and just disappeared through the crowd. It was all God and for His glory; you don't take credit for that.

At another time, I was driving back from San Francisco at about 5:30AM. I was with my two friends, who were asleep, driving my Lincoln Navigator SUV through some coastal area, when a 4-door sedan with two Latin guys passed me like I was standing still. Being a stunt driver, I observed the right-hand curve ahead of us. And I said to myself, "They're never gonna make it." I was still kind of mad that they cut me off, but it's something that, as humans, we gotta admit…when someone cuts us off, we kind of hope that they crash. And they did.

Their car rolled, and like Jerry Seinfeld, I said, "That's a shame." As the car rolled a few more times, I said, "Oh! That's gonna leave a mark!" When the car righted itself, the two imbeciles were dazed and confused. There was grass packed in the door jams of the car as they had rolled into a field. At that point, I had already thrown my car into park. My passengers woke up and they got to see the drive-in movie, starring me pulling out two morons who were going too fast!

By the time the car had landed right side up, it was smoking. The doors wouldn't open, so I grabbed them under their arms and pulled them out through the windows. They were Ok, but drunk for sure. I started to walk back down the center of the highway towards my SUV. Once I got back, I said on my cell, "That's right officer, its mile marker #142, and they are okay now. But I'd check them for DUIs." My friends were staring at me with their mouths open asking what just happened. I said, "Never mind. Hang around me enough and you'll get used to it."

I had been telling my friend Linda about my stories of pulling people out of car wrecks, which she sort of politely dismissed and said, "that's nice." I could have said I had three days to live for all she knew. Anyway, one day I was driving down the freeway into LA and I get a phone call from Linda. She told me that she was driving back home, but had felt funny. "Can you explain it? Do you have the flu?" She said no, that it was nothing like that. And then I told her to just be quiet. God took me into this prayer. I don't know why I prayed this at the time since I don't usually pray for people's cars, but I prayed for legions of angels to protect her and her car. No sooner that I got that out, I heard a bang on the other end. She said in a frantic voice, "I just had my rear tire blow out." I managed to ask, "Where are you?" to which she replied, "405 and 101." I heard her scream, followed by glass shattering and a car wrecking sick noise. Then the phone line went dead.

You're not gonna believe this, but as I was going over the 405 freeway on the 101, I looked to my right, and there was her tiny metallic blue Jaguar, partially pinned underneath a semi-tractor truck. We weren't supposed to meet that day and we didn't even know where each other was going to be. I threw my car in park and ran down the freeway. I was the first person there and was able to pull her out of the wreckage through the passenger side.

Well, it seems like that prayer was exactly what the doctor ordered… Dr. God that is. She had started to slide underneath the tractor trailer at a high speed, but the rear trunk of the car caught the back tire of the tractor trailer, keeping her car from going completely under and cutting her pretty little head off. Linda was a model, and I don't think there were too many calls for headless models. Out of 14 million people in the city of LA, I'm the first on the scene to pull her out of the wreckage. Yeah, "that's nice." After that day, when I had a story to tell her, she was all ears! She later confessed to me that she had a dream about me and what the future held for me. The dream was that I would preach the gospel and help many people.

CHAPTER 6

TIGERS, TRIGGERS AND TREATMENTS

A DECADE OF DECADENCE, destruction and dreams. It all started off at the party of the Century, year 2000 Millennium Party. Yup that's me, sitting next to the late Hugh Hefner at the one and only Playboy Mansion in Holmby Hills, California. I was also standing next to Hef and his entourage of Playmates at midnight during the countdown, but out of respect for the most wonderful woman of my life, my wife Lina, there's no need to show those pictures.

I sat down and asked Hef the question that every man would want to ask him, "What advice would you give me on women, for success?" He said, "When you meet a woman that you're interested in, be straight forward and tell them what you would like from them: I want to be friends with benefits, I'm looking for a girlfriend but I still want to date other girls, I want you to be my girlfriend, etc." The truth! How refreshing! Who would have thought? All these punks that wanna be playas lie to girls, and women know it. But sometimes they still put up with it. Ladies, wake up! You don't need to put up with that! Don't get played!

I found his advice to be very true. Women are extremely competitive, even moreso than men. So, when you tell them that you like them but still wanna date other women, they either get insecure or extremely competitive. That's about the time most women are willing to go further than the other woman to please you, to be the winner of the prize, only to dump you later. No, but seriously, it's just how life is. Life's too short for games.

Real men don't need to belittle women, control them or manipulate them. A lot of guys out there couldn't even handle one real woman. That's why you play a bunch of girls till they figure you out; then you keep it moving. Responsibility, and building a relationship with one amazing woman, is what makes a real man. Your life only gets better, and you become best friends and partners through life. You have to be on the same page. Life's tough enough without fighting and arguing with each other. And as far as playing with all the other girls, trust me, it doesn't make you more of a man. Besides, you'll save yourself a lot of time at the free clinic and not dying of AIDS and diseases!

It's also how God intended it to be. One man and one woman. Be fruitful and multiply. When you're together on the same page, you can

raise your family. You must treat your partner with the respect that you would want to be treated with, and all will go well. Adultery causes divorces, broken homes, troubled kids, jail time, drug and alcohol abuse., and plenty more. How do I know? Because I came from that kind of home. It never works that way!

For all you ladies out there, when some fool comes to you and says, "Hey, let's kick it. Let's hang out," they are basically saying, "I don't feel like spending money on you, but I wanna take advantage of you." Sex is a benefit of marriage. Understand? A BENEFIT. How you gonna walk up to a counter at IBM or Apple and say, "Hello ma'am, I hear your company has great benefits. I'd like some of them." The lady at the counter will tell you, "But Sir, you don't work here." So. the next time some guy asks you for some free benefits, since sex is a benefit of marriage and marriage takes work, a labor of love, you say to that fool "Oh, what you're really asking me for is that you'd like to fill out a job application." And that's how you go about it. You screen them as if they were a candidate for a job . If you have a dad, a grandfather, or a good uncle, have them help you with the screening. Just a little preaching there. Moving forward.

The start of 2000 introduced a hectic decade, but my dream of working with wild animals had just began to come into fruition. At that time in Hollywood, writers got greedy. They weren't snorting enough cocaine and wanted more money. In protest, the WGA, Writers Guild of America, started a strike and wanted SAG, Screen Actors Guild, to strike with them. So, we did, in support of their cause. They got what they wanted, but by the time we went back to work, we lost two years of prime-time TV to reality shows. When SAG went on strike the next year, what do you think the writers did? They said, "We hate actors. We're not gonna strike with you." At one point, I lost my house and had to live in a horse trailer the hills. Yeah that's right, a horse trailer.

That's how reality shows started to break into Hollywood. Every moron and his brother with a stupid idea started to get a show, and these guys were real idiots who had never worked in the industry. They treated people like shit, used everybody they could and spooned trash TV all over the world. That's why you see all this garbage like the Kartrashions, Jersey Hos, and that stupid Bruce Gender show. It was all completely idiotic, adding no value to anyone, anywhere. I can hear the brain cells of the people watching, frying like scrambled eggs. Add medical marijuana and Pokemon Go into the mix, and now you're a completely worthless metrosexual.

The days when I used to get paid $1,500-$2,000 in a day for doing stunts were far pas over. Now, union went to all of these cheap and cheesy reality show casting calls, where they wanted to pay $150 a day and they wanted you to do everything. I hadn't been getting far in my career, so I formulated a plan.

As I went to the castings, I became my own agent and prayed to God to get me gigs and be my manager. I'd rather give God the 15% than the lazy managers I've had (whose names aren't worth being mentioned).

But it started to work. I turned into an animal, calling it "Relentless Management". "Alex," the fast talking, New York accented manager, had become my altered ego; but it was really me. When I would go to the castings, the directors would complement my aggressive go-getter manager. I said, "Yes, he's quite the animal." They liked his style. Sounds schizophrenic, but it worked for both of us!

The union stuntmen didn't wanna take on the cheap and dangerous jobs, and told me not to either, saying I would make them look bad. I said, "Look. My daddy's not a famous stunt coordinator. And my uncle ain't Francis Ford Coppola." I had to do it on my own. By the way, that's a shot at Nicolas Cage cause that's how he got his start.

I had figured out a system. I went to the casting calls, and I was a Pitbull. I'd do 3-4 auditions a day. Other actors were lucky to get two auditions per week from their agents. I had my ADHD to thank for all the skills I had come to acquire. I was always active in experiencing and learning how to do different things, becoming well-rehearsed with stunts, weapons, wild animals, fight scenes, dialects, period piece stuff, cowboys, cops. My Jaguar worked (I listed my cars with castings), my three German Shepherds worked (I trained them as K9 cop dogs), my house worked… everything worked. Pimped it out!

The animal and horse companies were struggling with the cheap pay of the reality shows too, so I would say, "I'll be the host, I'll be the director, I'll be the line producer, I'll be the horse wrangler, I'll bring the horse, I'll ride the horse, fall off the horse, be the stuntman, be the stunt coordinator…everything but frickin' craft service. I will do it." So, in exchange, when I got them work, they would hire me as the host and the wild animal handler and trainer.

I worked with all sorts of animals, from Bengal tigers to Siberian tigers, leopards, full grown African lions, African elephants, two of the only white rhinos in captivity, jaguars, bears and monkeys. However, I didn't really enjoy working with monkeys. Monkeys are funky. One of our red-faced capuchin monkeys with little fangs, like in the movie the *Hang Over*, for no reason jumped off my shoulder, onto a newscaster lady, and tore half her ear off. You just never know what they'll do.

I don't mind telling you that I would sooner turn my back on anybody in Hollywood before I turned my back on any of these animals. They (Hollywood) were the true venomous vipers. Still to this day, there's a lot of people in Hollywood driving around in Mercedes, with bank accounts filled due to my work that they put their name on. That's kind of a regular thing in Hollywood, but that too will soon be gone, as China will eventually be buying all of Hollywood and the film industry, and they're not going to put up with that kind of stealing and BS. They don't care much for competition.

I was making $150-$200 times three or four roles in one day; it was working out for me. I became a consulting producer and worked with armorers since I was a weapons instructor. And God knows, the other candy-ass, wanna-be actors couldn't pull it off. There's something stupid about a GQ looking detective going into the hood to ask Crips and Bloods questions, you know? It looks stupid on TV and films.

I'll never forget the show I did with Jerry Springer, called *Baggage*. It was a dating show where you brought your baggage, meaning, whatever your problem was, and you would reveal it to the world. There were three guys and one girl. The girl was a substitute school teacher and a wanna-be actress, so they pretended she still was. And the other two guys had baggage, like one of them still lived in the basement of his mom's house and was trying to be a producer. I don't remember what the other chowder head guy had going on. They billed me as an End Time's survivalist living with pit-bulls and tigers in my house. All of which was mostly true.

In any case, the point was to impress the girl and win a date by belittling each other. There were a crew of girls that were cheering me on and kept telling the girl, "That one! Pick that one!" The other guys were just Hollywood smart asses, and in a war of wits and word battle, they were outgunned mental midgets. You see, I'm known by a nickname, "One Take," because I only need one take and my improv is sharp. And from being in jail and around Tupac, you'll undoubtedly get clowned if you try to diss me; and that's exactly what happened.

I won the date, and then we exposed our baggage. My baggage was that I smoked Cuban cigars inside the house. And that just wasn't P.C. (politically correct). Hers was that she wore adult diapers because she had a weak bladder. We decided if whether we could handle each other's baggage and carry on to the next date. Of course, for the sake of TV, we both said yes, but I had no real interest in dating her. She was a whiny JAP from New York, that stands for Jewish American Princess, and annoying as heck.

Our episode aired around the world and was rated #1. The producers called me and congratulated me and then said they had a problem. "We have to recreate your world." I said, "The world that the writers exaggerated and blew out of proportion, like that I live with 20 pit bulls, a tiger inside my house, and a full bomb shelter with weapons, gas masks and stored food… including elephants and other animals?"

I said. "That's not my problem. That's your problem." So, they said, "What will it take?" I told them. They said yes, so I started to line produce the episode, "Baggage First Dates." We pulled out all the stops. I took her to a wild animal game reserve, and worked with the animals, monkeys and elephants. The tiger was supposed to live at my house, so we took a 700-pound Siberian tiger to my friend's house where the horses were, and I found other friends who brought all of their pit-bulls. I brought in some of my weapons, freeze dried food and tactical gear, and we were able to set up a bunker.

So now it's go time. We shot the morning sequence with all the animals. Everything went great until the middle of the day, where the surprise was to take her to my horse stall, where Asia, the Siberian tiger, was waiting. She didn't know it was there. When I casually walked her around the corner, she shrieked and freaked out when she saw the tiger. I'm sure the tiger thought the same when it saw her.

The problem was that the attorneys for the TV show had done a bait and switch contract with us, where the contract basically said that if one of the key grips stubbed his toe, it was the tiger's fault. All bullshit. So, we got to the key part, and the contracts were still not right. We had 15 minutes to get everything started, and were losing daylight. The tiger was in the hot trailer for an hour, and you have to acclimate the tiger to its surroundings and let it cool off before you film. Otherwise, someone's gonna get hurt, and they strike at the ones closest to them. That'd be me!

Before we rolled, I called the attorneys in front of thirty people. They thought they were smug and said, "That's just how it has to be." So, I said to them "Well I'm not some highly intelligent 'Mr. Law' attorney like yourselves. I'm just a simple cowboy and an animal trainer, but check this out. We already shot most of this show. And if you don't correct this within the next 5 minutes, I'm gonna walk off this set, take the tiger with me, and you're gonna lose three days worth of footage. And you still need to pay the tiger because she'll get her meat one way or another. Handle it, or it's a wrap and you still owe us money."

Everyone looked at me like, oh boy, now you've done it. But I can tell you from dealing with some hardened characters, lawyers don't throw fear my way. Within one minute, we could all hear the fax machine in the other room from the attorney's office pumping out the correct contracts. Fancy that. They had them all along.

Now, when we went to roll camera and the actress came around the corner and shrieked, it set off the tiger, who then looked at me, came up to the bottom of my chest, pinned her ears back, spring loaded, and came at me with a giant paw to pull my arm into her mouth. I had just pulled my arm away fast enough to avert disaster. The other trainer and I rolled Asia on to her back and made her submit. Mandatory correction.

As this is occurring, the producers and directors on the other side of the bars ran, screaming at the top of their lungs, "Run Andre! Save yourself! Get out of there!" I just stood there calmly, lowered my heart rate and energy, which reflected onto the cat, and simply said into my microphone (to the producers and directors), "Can you all still hear me?" They replied, "Yes." And with a low tone and a growling voice I said, "Then shut the fuck up. You are ruining the scene. You are winding up this cat with your energy. And if I walk out of here now, I will never be able to work with this tiger again. She will get the better of me." They complied, and within an hour later, I was rolling around on the grass and bottle feeding the same tiger that tried to attack me. But this time, that tiger had respect for me…for not running off.

The rest of the day with the scenes turned out great, except for the fact that the actress was really starting to piss me off, as she was telling me how to act. She said, "You don't need to try so hard." I said, "You don't know what the heck you're talking about. I'm not an actor. I'm here being me, so with all due disrespect, I won't have you telling me how to be me."

Since she was so annoying, I had to return the favor in the next scene where we did the air-raid bunker. There was a red flashing light, like we were getting bombed. I put an annoying gas mask on my face that made me sound like Darth Vader, picked up the shotgun, pumped the shotgun over and over in a sketchy movement looking in all directions and said, "What was that?! What was that?! They're here! They're here! Did you hear that?!" I freaked her out. She kept saying "Stop it! Stop it!" She didn't want it to be funny, but it was. Everyone was laughing. She looked stupid, but she had it coming.

After that, I was a gentleman and cooked her a candle light dinner. Chicken piccata, chocolate dipped strawberries injected with Grand Marnier and creme brulee. So, I came out being the hero anyway. The producers said "Man, you need your own show dude." What had really happened here, I didn't realize at the time. God had been preparing me to produce, direct, and run my own production company.

I had to get an additional job to make ends meet because of the cheap reality show BS, so I worked at Wolfgang Puck's crown restaurant "Granita" in Malibu. I had also worked with Wolf at the Academy Awards Governor's

Ball after the Oscars, where he had done all the catering. He had also owned Spago in Beverly Hills, how he got his start, where I went one night after the Academy Awards and actually shared a lobster and broccoli pizza with the famous Donna Summer. I had worked at the Dorothy Chandler Music Center Pavilion Restaurant, where they held the Academy Awards. All I had to do was keep my tux on and go downstairs and, voila! I was one of them. The first people I met was Cheech Marin and Tommy Chong of *Cheech and Chong,* and they were my heroes. I grew up with their movies.

Then I met Sylvester Stallone, Dolly Parton, and the list goes on and on. It was the funniest thing because every time Cheech and Chong would see me, they would walk over and shake my hand and give me a hug. Cheech, with his East LA slang would say loudly, "Congratulations, Man!" like I'd won an Oscar. It made everyone wonder.

I had ended up at Granita, working with Wolf and Barbara, his wife at the time. Those were funny times too, and I thank God for them. I would clear $400-$500 cash a night in tips. Not only that, but I got to work with the world's biggest celebrities. I had become the VIP server at Granita that everyone would ask for.

For each dining experience, I got to direct guests through the meal and the wine selection, seating them at a great table if I wanted. We had a range of people on the guest list, from Dick Clark, Cuba Gooding Jr, Brendan Fraser, Barbra Streisand, Rob Reiner and James Cameron. I also had the chance to serve Diana Ross, who is a notoriously cheap tipper.

Once, Pamela Anderson had bailed me out at the restaurant. Wolf's assistant chef, Jennifer, was a real jerk when Wolf wasn't around. One night, Jennifer went off on me for serving the meal exactly how Pam had ordered it. Pam put her in check and made her cry. Thanks Pam. She was dating Kid Rock at the time, who would come in too. Mel Gibson, with his antique motorcycles, would stall out in the parking lot on cold foggy nights in Malibu. I had to go out and help him start his bikes. "Mel, buy a new bike, you can afford it," I would say.

During this time, Robert Downey Jr. was going through it, and boy was it a mess. One night, one of the customers came storming in and said "That's disgusting! You have a vagrant drunk passed out in front of your restaurant. Do something immediately, or I will." I had walked over and woken the man up. It was my friend Robert Downey Jr. After seeing him like that, I could have made $50,000 cash calling the Paparazzi or taking a picture of him looking that way, but I never would. I struggled from the same addictions. So instead, I helped him up. He said he was Ok to walk home, which was right down the block in Malibu Colony. I guess he wasn't all right, because that was the night he walked into his neighbor's house and went to sleep in the guest bedroom, thinking it was his house. It freaked the neighbor out. Anyway, I had seen Robert in there a couple of times. He reminded me of myself. He would walk into the bathroom and come back out to the booth zinging. When the edge of your nose starts to look like the rim of a salted margarita glass, it's time to stop. It was a pleasure to see Robert get sober and healthy again. I told him I would pray for him and that I struggled from the same thing. Now, I'm sober and healthier than ever. Maybe we will work on Iron Man 6 together.

One of the greatest impacts on my life came from the insult comedian of the century, Don Rickles. He was one of the original Rat Pack members from Las Vegas, you know, Dean Martin, Sammy Davis Jr, and Frank Sinatra. If you don't know, the original rat pack was started out of Humphrey Bogart's home in Beverly Hills. It was poker night. Bogart was known as the King and the rat pack leader, till he passed on. Bogart is one of my favorite actors. I looked up to these kinds of people growing up, as I had no one else to look up to. That's why it makes me sick when actors and pro-athletes allow themselves to look like complete morons when they abuse their wives, beating and cheating on them. They don't realize that little kids are looking up to them and emulating them!

Don Rickles would come in regularly and give me encouraging talks. He told me something that

I still carry with me every day. He said, "My brand of humor was hated. I wasn't P.C...Everyone told me to knock it off. Everyone criticized me. But I'm gonna tell you what I told myself. Never give up. Doesn't matter what anyone says about you. Stay persistent always. Stay..." and I interjected, "Relentless?" He said, "Exactly!"

But it was James Cameron that really got me to where I am now. First, he came in and I would serve appletinis to him and his wife. They would bring their baby in and he would have a glass of wine with dinner. After getting to know him, he told me that director Walter Hill was his mentor. I said, "Walter gave me my start in Wild Bill." I continued, "As you are going to be my mentor?" Tall talk, for a waiter carrying an appletini.

I said to myself, "One day I'm gonna get out from around this table and be on set with these people." I worked at Granita Malibu because, as an aspiring actor, I could hide out there. I wouldn't want to be a waiter in Hollywood or Beverly Hills. Too many people would see you. I guess in a way, we all want to pretend that we never had to do work like this. That's for you, David Schwimmer of "Friends", who was a waiter too at one time.

Meanwhile, back at the ranch, I had gone to donate blood at the Red Cross, as I liked to do. It was easier than donating blood on set as a stuntman. One day I received a certified letter from the Red Cross. Ouch, that can't be good. I opened the letter and it notified me that I had liver cancer. The letter urged me to go to a doctor right away. So, I did what anybody in denial would do; I threw the letter away.

Ignoring the second and third letters, I kept telling myself, "I'll be fine." I lasted almost two years without going to the doctor; then I hit a wall. I had collapsed and had been taken to the ER, where I had been so many times before for various craziness and stunts gone wrong. I should have had my own parking spot, as I'd walk in the door and was greeted by name, like Norm when he walked into "Cheers". When you're a local celebrity at your ER, that can't be good. Unfortunately, this was not something they could re-set, throw a bandage on, or give me a shot for. This was serious and terminal.

They ran some tests and proved true what Red Cross had already informed me of. It was terminal liver cancer. I had jaundice, fatigue and couldn't even walk around without feeling like I just ran a marathon. I felt 20 years older than I was and my liver was shutting down. I looked the way I felt, as you will see in the pictures of me then, compared to the pictures of me now. I was slowly dying, and it showed.

I went to another doctor, who gave me the same diagnosis. I went to a third doctor. He said, "There just isn't a treatment for this. There are some drugs that may prolong your life for a little while, but there's no cure for this."

I was at the door, preparing to leave the office of the last doctor, when I heard a nurse say under her breath, "Andre, come here. I'm not supposed to be telling you this, but there is a doctor in Beverly Hills at Cedars-Sinai Medical Center who is looking for experimental patients, to be basically a guinea pig, for a new treatment." I took his number and called him, setting an appointment to see him.

Once I was there, the doctor had walked in with 2 nurses and asked me what I did for a living. I said, "I do stunts, work with wild animals, explosives, and crash cars for a living. Why?" As I sat there reading my Bible, he said, "This is gonna be a dog fight." I replied, "It won't be mine. It will be God's." "There is great risk." I laughed and replied, "So? I just got off the 405 freeway at rush hour. That was a bigger risk." He liked my attitude. He and the nurses went into the other room, talked and came back out. He said, "You are just who we're looking for."

You see, they couldn't take an old woman or man, or anyone that was weak-minded. It was a couple of years of treatment, constant in and out of the hospital and injections almost every day of the week. As I signed up, I asked him, "What's my other option?" He said, "Pretty much a cold box, 6 feet under". I told him I'd rather fight.

I checked into the hospital for the first couple of weeks. They started the multiple treatment injections and kept drawing my blood every 4 hours to test it. The main floor nurses at Cedars-Sinai could not know what was going on since it was an experiment. They would just come in very kind and say, "We can't know what you're in here for, but we know it's serious if we can't know. But you are so quiet and calm, and never ask for anything or need anything." They said they had people on their floor complaining constantly.

I always had my Bible open, and I remember saying to God "God, if you want me to come home, I'm good with that. But if you get me out of this one, I'll stay here, serve you and give the devil a headache every day, for the rest of my life." At this point, I reflected on decades of drug abuse and alcoholism. There's probably a cocaine field in Bolivia named after me, and a giant statue of myself in front of the Puerto Rican rum factory after how much money I'd spent. Buy hey, what I can say.

I was trying to collect disability, considering I'd been paying into the system and started working earlier than the age of 15. But no, no disability for me. I wasn't the right colored skin or minority. Actually, the government knew I was going to die, so I guess they figured there was no point in helping me out. It made me mad to go into a doctor's office with my medical kit, full of different meds and syringes, feeling sick and looking yellow, but being denied for disability. When walking to the doctor's office, I would see healthy looking African Americans in their 20s, smoking joints with younger Latin Americans, going to the same doctor's office stoned and claiming that they had some sort of back pain. Then they'd walk out of the office, laughing and bragging about the checks and benefits they were collecting. So, this isn't "haterade." It's the truth…I couldn't get a penny to save my life!

It was at that point that I got introduced to Interferon, a medication which is extremely brutal on the mind and body. They made me sign a medical disclosure for that read, "May cause homicidal and suicidal thoughts." Boy, they weren't kidding. After they dosed me, it was like the worst hang over combined with the worst flu, with body cramps, cold sweats and dry heaves all at once for about 4-5 days in a row! Right when I would start to come out of it, I would have to inject again. Nice, huh? The stuff made me feel exactly what they said, giving me an edge, quite literally. I was driving around LA with a razor-sharp samurai sword, hoping someone would cut me off. Thank God that didn't happen!

Since Uncle Scam, I mean, Uncle Sam wasn't going to pay me, I needed to work. But how am I gonna work like this? Lots of prayers. Believe it or not, I got cast on a show called "Extreme Animal Control" at Paramount Studios and was on contract for 6 months. It was perfect timing. And guess what my job was? I was the host and carnivore expert. That means I'm supposed to be wrangling live tigers and lions. All the while, still on Interferon. YAY!

They asked me to set up the scenes, and again, here I am producing stuff without producer's pay. So, I gave my good friend, Randy Miller, a call. He was one of the craziest and best tiger and lion trainers, along with my good friend Hayden from A-Z Animals. Those two were best in the industry. Randy had made a name for himself, training his tigers, lions and grizzly bears too hot…which means wild and close to the edge to get the predators in action shots. Randy's cousin had been killed on film by a grizzly bear, owned by Randy, and it went viral. Poor Randy. If it wasn't enough to lose his cousin, but they had to keep showing it everywhere!

Hollywood, the bunch of hypocrites that they are, didn't agree that lions, tigers, horses and other animals should be on TV and film. But yet, they all want them and pay for them. Just like guns. They don't indorse the NRA. They talk shit and put an anti-American President in office that doesn't support the 2nd amendment, but make billions off of violent gun movies. To them, I just say, "Shut up, Stupid! Yeah, you heard me." I grew up under the Hollywood sign and was born in Hollywood Presbyterian Hospital. Raised in the industry, so I have every right to say what I want.

Most of Hollywood didn't even come from Hollywood. Just a compilation of libtards around the world.

If you haven't guessed it by now, I'm all American and all about God, Family, Country, Morals and Values. I back our Military and Law Enforcement, and all our 2nd Amendment Patriots. God bless America forever! If you don't like it, you might as well close the book now because I'm not done talking. But if you hang in there, you might learn something, and I'll prove my point. I'm all about facts.

My grandma came to Hollywood from Yugoslavia after barely surviving two world wars, where most of her family, including her mom, and her brothers, were killed by Nazis. She was a true warrior. My grandma, Mileva Petrovitch, was about 5-foot-tall in stature, but a spiritual giant. She said the only thing that got her through all of those hard times of war was classic Hollywood movies, MGM musicals and 20th Century Fox. I was raised on I love Lucy, John Wayne movies, Humphrey Bogart's black and whites...the classics. And I appreciate that. That's why I hate the trash coming out of Hollywood now, and what its influence has done to this once great Nation.

So, I'm half Yugoslavian, half Russian, but all American. Mileva came at a time when you do it legally by taking an oath, getting your green card properly and respectfully, and showing pride to be an American. At that time, America was the land of opportunity and dreams, where anyone with hard work and a will could make anything they wanted out of their lives. That was the America I grew up in and loved!

Her personality was always upbeat, always outgoing and positive. I would always see a little candle in a red container burning while she was praying. She prayed a lot and I always wondered what she was talking to God about. I reckon a lot of it was me. She spent the most amount of time with me. When everyone else had counted me out, she never did. She loved me more than anybody most of my whole life. She was an inspiration. But back to Randy.

Randy had moved up to Big Bear, California so that he could have all his wild animals in cooler temperatures, rather than in the rest of the California heat. Good move on Randy's part since Siberian tigers and grizzly bears are used to forests and cold weather. Randy had won the Stuntman of the Year award, and helped Russell Crowe win the Oscar for *Gladiator*. Randy had been under that wig, getting attacked by 2 tigers, not Russel. But Russel did a great job and gave two thumbs up to Randy.

I called Randy and we set up the shooting schedule for the TV show. Since I was the carnivore expert, I picked the cat. I picked Taboo, the largest

African male lion (with an attitude) that ever worked on Hollywood films and TV. The week before we had filmed part of

"Extreme Animal Control," the production company didn't want to spring for a real full-sized python, so they used a giant rubber one and then a smaller real python and tried to cheat the shot. I said, "Oh hell no! I can't believe you're gonna put me in a project like this." I wanted to make sure that we had real lion footage, not real LYING footage!

We went up to Randy's to film our recreation show. Here was the "gag," as we call it in the stunt world. An old German lion trainer had lived in the desert, and every time he would leave his house, since it was in the middle of nowhere, these tweakers, aka meth addicts, kept breaking into his house. So, he did what I would do, putting his lion in the house. When they broke in again, they barely made it back out to their truck. They were freaking out and couldn't even find the keys to put into the ignition.

The giant lion jumped up and down on the hood, denting it and ripped the windshield wipers off, breaking the glass. It was just about to pull them out like a couple of sardines in a can, when the police showed up, ready to shoot the lion. Then the "Extreme Animal Patrol" and I, regulation and carnivore expert extraordinaire, came to their rescue. So, my job here is to get Taboo off the hood of the truck while he is freaking out.

We put low voltage wires around the perimeter and we got ready to film. That's when the director, the same director that liked to use large fake rubber snakes, told me not to take a chance and step over the hot wire or go near the lion if I didn't have to. They said, "Cheat the shot". I replied, "Ha! Okay Sir." When I walked over to Randy, he could see I was a little upset. I told him about the little charade that had been going on and what the director told me. Then, I looked at Randy and said, "We will not be filmed like that. And we aren't going out like wussies." Randy laughed and said, "Hell yeah!"

The camera rolled and it was a super-hot day. I knew I had one take and nobody nearby to help me. I was out in the open and in Taboo's territory. When the director's yelled "Action!" that's what I gave them. I remember stepping over the trip wire on purpose, but felt myself getting dizzy. Oh no, Mr. Interferon was kicking in. I was so dizzy that I was seeing double and triple.

Then I heard Randy's voice, "Hey! Come get your cat!" I heard the rest of the crew, and my co-host, Christian Billings, one of the best in the industry and a great friend, say, "What the heck is he doing?" and everyone else was yelling and tripping out. I went and poked Taboo on the butt, with a stick. That was his cue to turn around and attempt to attack me. I guess my cues and Randy's are different. Taboo turned around so fast, roared at me and took a swat at the stick from atop a 4-wheel-drive hood, which was even worse for me. All he had to do was jump down on top of me!

I just stayed calm, remembering when Asia tried to attack me. Freaking out or running was not an option. You only turn into prey, or meals on wheels. As he jumped off the hood of the car, he began to lower his head. Not a good sign. That meant he was stalking. I used as much confidence as I could to start walking backwards toward the trailer and get away from all three lions I had been seeing.

I started to bang on the trailer door and ordered him to go in. Taboo stopped and just stared at me. I had thrown my last piece of meat and he wasn't interested in it. I swiftly went around to the trailer door, which was steel bars in a cage, and started to swing it towards him. Randy had told me that if anything goes wrong, to just try and get on top of the trailer. He said, "We will see if we can get to you in time." Thank God Taboo got into the trailer. Right after he did, I leaned against the gate just as Taboo lunged and rattled the shit out of it. Good thing Randy warned me to lock it down as soon as I closed it. Most people don't and the cat gets mad and charges out, as he had done before.

In case you'd never been near a real lion, when it roars, it's like the ground trembles, and it's unbelievably powerful. In that instance, your blood just gets cold. After that, I took a little walk towards the forest, telling the crew that I needed to use the restroom; but really, I was just sick. Nobody could know that I was on Interferon or any medications. The footage turned out amazing. However, as predicted, the stupid rubber snake killed the show. Thanks a lot, stupid director.

I had been a shooter since I was a little kid. My first dad's best friend, Birka, was one of the leading competition shooters in the LAPD. This was the time that the Dirty Harry magnum movies, starring Clint Eastwood, were huge, and Clint had always been an idol to me. Later in life, I got to work with him in person. Birka was a serious shooter. He collected guns. My grandfather used to take me out to the desert to teach me how to shoot. As part of being an American, guns were just part of the USA. It was only later that the wrong idiots with guns gave it a bad name.

A special thanks to the NRA for doing it the right way and defending our constitution and our Nation. I had been working with guns a long time in the industry. As a stuntman, they'd rather use somebody that knows real guns, even if we are using blanks, as opposed to some wimpy looking guy blinking his eyes and looking scared of the gun while he's shooting it. I applied for every one of those castings that I could. In fact, I made a good career out of it and got jobs over other actors because of my real-life gun experience.

I had worked with the United States Marine Corps, training in aggressor role and playing at Two Nine Palms, where we dress like terrorists, grab

AKs and fire live rounds on the other side of the wall from the Marines. Our military wanted the boys to know what it really felt like to be shot at and hated for no reason. I was happy to back our military at all times.

That led me to further work. Real, and on-camera. My second dad Rae Williams, God rest his soul, had moved out to Arizona in the middle of nowhere on a dirt highway, an hour away from any main towns. He stated and managed a private military gun range and airport on the Arizona Mexico border, where Special Ops, SEAL teams, Snipers, Marine Corps, Border Patrol and Federal Agents were trained.

It was there that my dad met Mike Dillon of *Dillon Aero* Minigun, only a machinist at that time. Mike was flying overhead and dropping little homemade bombs in the desert in a Cessna over my dad's property (just for amusement). The property was huge and all desert, so there were no fences and markers. Dad waved him down and Mike landed on his private airstrip.

My brother Al had just come back from the pentagon and had a problem. We needed to strip some weight off the then utilized U.S. government minigun, that kept jamming and proved to be problematic in Vietnam. Upon arriving to the desert, my dad introduced Al to his new friend, Mike Dillon. Al said, "What do you do for a living, Mike?" Mike said replied that he was a mechanist. Al said, "Maybe you can help me with a problem." Not only had Mike fixed the jamming problem on the minigun, but he stripped 28 pounds of unnecessary weight off. It was performed amazingly after that. He pulled his own patents and the Dillon Aero Minigun took off big time, and all because of a little desert meeting between a couple of patriots.

I remember work getting slow in Hollywood. I was still sick and dying, yet I loaded up my pickup truck with my guns and my German Shepherds, and went out to Arizona to work. It was about 110-115 degrees out there, and with the Interferon injections, it was brutal at best. I worked with Sikorsky Black Hawk crews, and Slick, the top Pilot at

Dillon, with two tours in Vietnam, training our military on the use of the 50-caliber machine gun and the Dillon 134D. While the Black Hawks were landing for reloading, we fly over and spray the armored vehicles and the cars that were set up inside the berms of the ranch (training for warfare in the Middle East). It was such a rush that it made me forget about my pain.

I would salute the choppers as they left for the day, but work wasn't over yet. They would spray rounds of tracers, which are ultraviolet rounds of red and violet colored ammo, along the Mexican border as they left, because when it got dark, the games begun.

Round two. The drug cartel moves in with its coyotes and mules. Mules are the people who want to get into America and are willing to carry the drugs across the border in the middle of the night. The coyotes are the dirty guys that work for the drug cartel and drive the mules. The only problem was, sometimes after the mules were done doing their job and made it across to freedom in America, they would get killed by the coyotes. They would leave them dead in the middle of the desert.

I started spotting for the US Border Patrol. Low flying planes would drop parcels at sunset with transponders in them. The drug cartel would pick them up on the other side, our side. So, it was for me to spot and give the coordinates early in the morning to the Border Patrol, when they staged their raids from my dad's place.

I remember going out to the gun range at sunset with those beautiful Arizona sunsets, feeling so peaceful. In addition to the money I was getting paid from the Sikorsky Black Hawk Dillon ventures, I also went out to do something called raking brass. Brass, especially 50 cal, was worth a lot of money, and it was laying there like some sort of gold veins in the ground. I knew our flight patterns, so I would just go out there with guns attached to my ATV like a modern-day cowboy, start raking brass, putting it into huge containers and selling it to the recycling place. You could make $600-$1500 a day cash just doing that!

Why with my guns? Because when it started to get dark and the choppers left, you could feel the eyes on you. The cartel had people as spotters too, and I wasn't going down without a fight.

One morning, the Border Patrol staged its raid on the coordinates I had given them and found a giant hay bale-sized parcel of dope. There had been people who have picked up huge amounts of cash with parcels like these, however, you learn never to touch it as it has transponders on it, just like in the movie *No Country for Old Men*.

While the Border Patrol was on the ground, dad and I would go up in his little Cessna to do some re-con and spotting work to see which direction, if any, the mule train and cartel went. These guys were such disrespectful pigs! They'd leave campsites littered with trash and smoldering rocks spelled out "EAT ME" that you could read from the sky. That's why I don't care much for being PC. There's no such thing. It's just being ignorant or wanting to listen to what the government wants to inform you through the lying liberal media.

After days of shooting, dad and I would go to the local bar and get a well-deserved pitcher of beer and some wings. My dad, in his Long Island accent, knew more jokes than Dillon had ammo. By the time I would return from the restroom, he would have the cocktail waitresses and female bartender all around him going, "He's such a cute old man!" Nonsense! He was doing his "wolf in sheep's clothing" routine and luring them all in. But thanks dad! Learned a lot.

We also filmed "Triggers", a Minigun Episode at dad's ranch. I was the co-host, stunt coordinator, weapons expert and consulting producer for the Military Channel. It was still during the time that I was sick and dying, but I felt like I was doing something good for God, Family, Country and our Military. It was good for my soul.

It was after the filming that I left the Arizona desert, but not for the last time. I had shown dad a thing or two about tenacity, but this was a guy who had been in the Air Force, been hit by a train, been a pilot and a pilot instructor, crashed plans, and managed to walk away from all of it. He was one of the toughest men that I knew. He taught me a lot about life and being tough, and loved me like I was his real son. My dad came from the WWII era, where people were proud to defend and protect America. Working hard was a good thing, and men were men and women were women, and they stayed that way!

Towards the end when dad had died, the stupid Obama administration had opened our borders. That first night, there were coyotes dressed in camo tactical gear and 25 people were loading up two tractor trailers full of dope on dad's property. The Border Patrol had been chasing them all through the desert. It was sad to see because for years, we had defended those borders against dope, terrorists, and 72,000 illegal aliens crossing. 12,000 come from the Middle East and they ain't bringing Christmas presents in those boxes! And now, you open the borders wide open and tell me there's nothing to worry about? Bullshit. If you believe that nothing bad is gonna happen, then I got a bridge to sell you!

I'd like to give special thanks to the United States Military, Dillon Aero, The Dillon Family, all of our Law Enforcement and the Border Patrol, who have done a great job in keeping America safe. It has got to be hard for you guys and your families to defend a nation and an administration (Obama) who doesn't care about defending our nation, but rather, only sabotaging it. God bless you, and may He keep you and your families safe too!

Shortly after returning to LA, I had gotten a call from the doctor's office, telling me that they needed another blood test. Two weeks later, they called me in for yet another blood test, but wouldn't tell me why.

I'll never forget, the night prior, when I was going through it on the Interferon in cold sweats. I felt like I was going to die right then, but was beyond calling for an ambulance or wanting any help. I figured I was just gonna go. All of a sudden, while laying in a pool of sweat on the bed, the fever just broke. Everything left me. I was laying there in peace at 4AM. I reckon that's when God performed the miraculous because that is when I felt everything leave my body. And in that moment, I was healed. However, it wasn't confirmed for a while.

When I did go back in for the second blood test, the doctors, with all serious expressions on their face, announced to me that they couldn't find it. I said, "Oh, it's an *it* now." They couldn't find any traces of the cancer, and said, "Congratulations, you're healed." I asked, "Would you put that on paper?" They said, "Normally we can't, but we are so sure, that for you we will." They had told me that they had pumped me full of the highest doses of Interferon they could because they knew I could handle it. Wow...thanks a lot.

I didn't know how to take that, except to say that now they know how much to dose people "so that others may live," which, by the way, is a saying by the PJs (Para-rescue of the United States Air Force Special Operations), who drop in behind enemy lines in dangerous situations by parachute, in any condition, to rescue people "so that others may live". A saying I got from my brother Al, a PJ for 35 years+.

CHAPTER 7

NOTHING TO LOSE YOUR HEAD OVER

FTER MY MIRACULOUS HEALING, I was still feeling pretty weak, especially in my wallet. I didn't have much money left and was bummed out, trying to regain my footing in this world. The government still refused me compensation. I had just gotten done struggling with a crack cocaine addiction and was trying to stay out of Compton, Inglewood and downtown LA.

Whatever the addiction, cocaine, meth, alcohol…I've been through it, and it's a powerful demon that grips you and only God can break its grip.

I would have a cigar with the boys at the Westlake Cigar Shop, watch TV and pretend that I was just like one of them. But at the end of the night, when the owner, my good friend Teddy, would lock up, I would go and park my car behind the shop and sleep in the alley. I had spent my last bit of money, paying for my friend Viva and her daughter to stay at a Motel 6 for a week; her daughter was a little toddler named Heaven. Viva had lost her father in a horrific horse accident and subsequently, they lost the family home. Viva had to be out on the street in her car with her daughter, and I couldn't allow that.

But, it was Ok since there was a loading area in the back of the cigar shop. Somebody had recently tried to break in to the stores through there. So, Teddy said, "If the sheriffs say anything, give them my phone number, and tell them you're my security." Now, if you know anything about Ventura County, their slogan is "Come on vacation, leave on probation." The sheriffs there don't play. But for me, even an alley in Ventura County in the middle of the night felt a lot less dangerous than midday in downtown LA or Compton.

One day, I got a phone call from Viva. She told me that she booked one of her first assignments with a detective agency and the Burbank Police. She had just gotten her license to carry a Glock 19, however, she was petite, attractive and not very street smart, so I asked her what the assignment was. She said it was a kidnapping ring and she was going to be the money drop girl to get a wealthy man's teenage daughter back. Nobody really knew the details, but we all found out later. It was much bigger than what we expected.

I told Viva that I had been trained in work like this by Howard Hughes' personal detective, and that I had also worked with law enforcement. Plus, I had been on those streets. Viva told me that she needed to make the drop on Sunset and Western the night of the 4th of July. I told her, "Are you kidding me? I know that corner. It's nothing but crackheads and gangsters. And you're gonna stand out there in a dress and heels with a bag of money?! They're gonna snatch you up and kidnap you too." Especially with what she was wearing, there was no place to hide a Glock so she would have to leave it in the car.

I told her to call the detective and guaranteed her that on the 4th of July, he would be short-staffed, and this would be dangerous. I instructed her to tell him that I would assist for free, just to make sure she was okay. Heaven had already lost a grandfather, it wouldn't be good to lose her mom too. Viva called me back 10 minutes later and she said, "I can't believe it. Everything you told me was right. Dale wants to meet you."

We all met at the Burbank Police Department at 5pm for a briefing. I got there early and met with Dale, who was a 40-year veteran detective of the LAPD. He asked me, "So what's your deal?" I told him that I had worked with the US military, that I was an ex-drug dealer, that I had done drug busts, helped solve murder cases inside of jails and that I could handle myself on the streets from weapons to self-defense. At that point, Dale's team of officers and Viva had arrived. There was Dale, four other guys, Viva, and myself. He put a map on the center of the table and said, "This is where we're gonna be. This is where the money drop is gonna take place, where the exchange will happen." I stood up over the map and asked, "May I?"

I pointed to the center of the map and said, "I know this corner very well (in fact I'd even bought dope there a few times). At that time of night, especially on the 4th of July, that corner will be hard to watch because you will have incoming boogies from every direction; meaning, all sorts of people to look out for, all at one time, and they are all gonna be sketchy looking people." I told Dale, "There's a bus bench there with a covering so I'll take position there. That way I can get to Viva fast if I need to."

Dale turned to Viva and said, "It's your ass. What do you want?" She said, "Yes, I wanna have Andre there for back-up". He then proceeded to break us up in teams and everyone had a partner except me and Viva. Her job was to drive her Mercedes up to the corner alone. At that point, the undercover badges were all issued, and I got a badge. Finally.

Anyway, weapons check time. Everyone had one except for me. I asked Dale if he would provide me with an extra one, but he wouldn't allow it. I didn't have a permit to be in possession of a concealed weapon anyway. I was authorized by the law to risk my life, but not authorized to defend it. Ok, I'll just have to do it another way. We all got ear pieces. I got the tiniest ear piece, so it was well hidden, and a tiny microphone on the inside of my shirt. I told them that I wanted to be dropped off early and walk in from half a mile away, to get a good feel and look at everything.

You want to "feel" the streets, get the flow of traffic. It's almost like a smell of instinct. I had been there so many times that I could actually sense if anything was unusual. Sounds crazy, but it's real. Dale and the other officers took their positions in their vehicles. Even though they were in unmarked cars, they had sirens and blue lights built into the grills of the cars and sirens. When they hit the switch and lit them up, you definitely knew that they were police!

As I proceeded to walk to the bus stop, I went right to the nearest trash can, I got lucky. I found an old beer bottle and a cigarette butt next to it on the ground. As I was down on the ground, I smeared my palm on the dirty pavement and wiped my face with it. I also had an old cap on backwards, showed up with a dirty old Pendleton and came unshaven (since I had been sleeping in my car). When I reached the bus stop, I laid down under the bench with my beer bottle and cigarette, blending in and looking like a homeless person on the street.

I heard a crackle in my ear piece. It was Dale. "Boy, you really look the part". I heard another officer say, "Doesn't look like it's your first time." I couldn't laugh too hard, I couldn't break from character. But yeah, that was it. Here comes Viva and she parks her Mercedes on the corner. There were a couple of other cars there and she had the money bag with her. Between you and me, I later found out that it was all just cut up newspaper, which was even more dangerous. If the kidnappers would have opened it, they would have taken Viva with them for sure!

Suddenly, I saw the kidnap victim walking down the street and a SUV following her. The following was supposed to occur: She was supposed to meet Viva, the kidnappers would get the money, and the girl would get into the Mercedes. I informed the detectives, "Suspects are in view". I could see a lot more from my angle than where the officers were sitting. We were still not sure whether the girl was really trying to escape, or was in on it, trying to get money from her dad, or strung along on drugs.

She was about 19 years old, very pensive and sketchy looking. The SUV that following her stayed at a distance. She was walking on my side of the street, almost to the bus bench heading towards Viva. All of a sudden, she ran across the street and just stood there. What we came to find out was that while we were in the parking lot watching the suspects, they had been in a car in the parking lot, watching us. So, they flagged the girl and didn't give her the green light to pick up the money. Things were getting tense, and we were so close, but yet so far!

The girl then ran into a Rite Aid Pharmacy that was on her side of the street, and the kidnappers pursued her, while some remained in the parking lot. I guess she thought she was going to get out through the back of the store. That was about the time all hell broke loose and Dale yelled, "Move! Go! Go! Go!" We didn't exactly have a plan for what was about to happen. Most of the time, in these kind of situations, nothing goes as planned. So, you have to rely on instinct. I jumped up, yelled at Viva to get in her car, lock it up and get her gun. Then I took off across the street.

The kidnapper's car tried to leave the parking lot, but was cut off by the officers. The girl ran out of the Rite Aid with one guy still chasing her. A younger officer, who was faster than me, started on foot pursuit toward the girl. I thought, "He's got this for sure!" While I'm running behind the younger officer, he jumps out into the street and somehow his knee goes out. I couldn't believe it! All of this was happening in the middle of two-way traffic on Western Boulevard, with no stop signs or stop lights. Dale comes sliding in sideways in his car and saved the younger officer's from being run over. So, I'm thinking, "Do I help them, or just advance on my own?" I went on my own. This was like the frickin' movie *Lethal Weapon* or something.

The girl, and the kidnapper, ran into the close-by apartment buildings, which had curved spiked fencing so no one could climb over. They had somehow managed to get into the building, but had shut and locked the gate. I then figured that they could be running out the back of the building, so I started to run around and noticed that there was a wall in front of me. I grabbed the rod iron fencing, using the wall to launch me over the fence. I was able to get in. I then heard the other officers yelling, "Open the gate, Andre!"

After opening the gate and letting the officers in, we all ran to the back, where they were cornered. "Get on the ground," the officers yelled to the criminals. Since I had handcuffs, I made the arrest and cuffed the suspects. In the meantime, the other officers were able to concentrate on the other car and stop those suspects as well, but the ones we apprehended were the main ones. Most importantly, our primary concern was to get girl out, safe and alive, and that's exactly what we did.

We then drove back to the Burbank police station; I rode in the car with Dale and the suspects. I turned to the suspects while in the car and said, "What were you thinking? That we wouldn't be able to get you?" They looked at me and replied, "Ha! Like we didn't know you were a cop under that bus bench." "Ha! I guess you didn't know fast enough. Look where you're sitting now!" I leaned into them and laughed!

Once we got to the police station, we took them into booking. As we walked through the glass doors, I caught a glimpse of myself in the glass with a badge on, and thought, "Wow. I guess God can use anyone." Then I told Viva to grab the back of the handcuffs, while I held onto the suspects under the arm from the back, so that she could officially walk them in.

By then, the kidnapped girl's father had showed up. He was so happy to have his daughter back. He would have never seen her again if this arrest wasn't made. Dale explained to the father what happened and the officers pointed to me and said, "He did it." The father looked at me said, "You! I kind of had a good feeling about you, when I saw you." He then pulled me aside and said, "I wanna give you $1,000 as a reward." I told him no. "It's in the line of duty." The father also offered $1,500 to have the suspects extradited. We had to extradite them to Arizona, and the father had asked me to do the driving. I said, "I know Arizona well, and that border too. I'll take that drive for $1,500."

Dale had later approached me and said, "Hey man. Can I talk to you? My boys have worked this case for a couple of weeks and put in surveillance time, away from their families. You did an amazing job, but they really need the money." I said, "I understand. That's cool. I'll stand down." What we later found out about this case was shocking. These guys had 3 other blonde teenaged girls kidnapped in a Hollywood hotel room. They had been stringing them out on drugs and had promised them that they were going to take them to Paris to be models.

These guys were from Saudi Arabia, and they had been putting out fake castings doing this before. They had no contacts or connections with the modeling world. They were going fly the girls into the Middle East and put them into underground brothels, as in prostitution slavery, where they would be sodomized and raped by 100 Mid-Eastern men a DAY until they were considered too old and would have their throat slit!

These suspects had been ruthless, and they told the girl that if she ran from the money exchange, they would slit the throats of the other 3 girls. That explained her strange behavior from earlier. On top of that, if she didn't make a clear getaway, they would have apprehended her again and tortured her and the other girls!

The Saudi Arabian authorities were notified that we had their people. They requested that we not incarcerate or put them through our American courts and jail system. The Saudi government assured us of swifter judgement. So, the criminals were put on a plane with proper officers, and (I LOVE this part!) as soon as these Mid-Eastern assholes got off the plane, they were immediately beheaded publicly on the tarmac. And you know what? I was glad to be a part of it. Once I found out the kind of guys they were…they could have been saved the plane trip. I would have beheaded them on the tarmac here and saved them fuel!

CHAPTER 8

ME & THE MASTERS OF MARTIAL ARTS

IT WAS THE 70S AND THE MOVIE *Enter the Dragon* came out, with my hero and idol at the time, Bruce Lee. I was practicing Kung Fu with my neighbor Dave, whose parents were sending him to a Kung Fu dojo. I wanted to join, but my parents wouldn't let me because of the money. So, I trained with Dave who also idolized Bruce Lee. I remember the influence he had on my life after seeing his amazing skills in *Enter the Dragon*, and later watching him on an interview where he said, "Be like water." Water assumes the shape of the container. It can flow over and through rocks, but can also pound and crush as well. Those words resonated with me.

I also recall the scary guy named O'Hara in the movie, who was Bruce Lee's nemesis that had a big scar across his face. In the movie, Bruce Lee made it a point to fight and brutally kill O'Hara, but with that Bruce Lee style. With a clenched fist and an intense body, he jumped up in the air and crushed O'Hara's wind pipe. His flying kick landed O'Hara on the ground; however, O'Hara was badass himself and was punishing and killing people up until that point.

This movie came out around the time that Bruce Lee had died. We were all in shock. The flame on the so brightly lit candle of Bruce Lee's life was snuffed out way too early in his life. In our eyes, he had just gotten started, but the legend, and his legacy continues and amplifies around the world. Below is a picture that I keep on my wall that reminds me of Bruce Lee and his attitude towards training. He was RELENTLESS.

Dave and Dan, a friend who lived across the street, were training one day. We had seen a vacant property in the neighborhood. All the houses were one level ranch-style, and about an acre. It was a great time to grow up in the San Fernando Valley, south of the Boulevard. Each of the houses, at one point or another, were horse properties and had old stables. The house that was vacant was next to a red barn style house that belonged to the "Lone Ranger". "Hi-Ho Silver!" he would yell. He had silver bullets and wore a black mask. He was a famous TV show star and an idol to a generation of kids.

That vacant house was finally bought. We saw a truck drop off some boxes and other stuff, and then nobody was there for a couple of weeks. We were curious kids, so we went and peeked through the window. We had seen a really cool European type motorcycle; I think it was a Sachs. Anyway, we loved motocross and were going from riding our minibikes, to our Schwinn bikes that we had transformed. We were the original BMXers, completed remodeling our Schwinn Stingray bikes. We replaced the banana seats with 10 speed bicycle seats, and took the handle bars down to the Midas muffler shop to be replaced with a welded cross bar. All the BMX bikes you see now are prototypes of ours. You owe us a lot of money!

We would watch Evel Knievel jump cars with his motorcycle and we emulate his style. We would haul ass down our hill, using a door on a metal trash can to see how many other trash cans we could jump...like Evel Knievel. And yes, we would eat shit just like he did at Caesars Palace. We were bloody and scabbed up little maniacs. But hey, it was the 70s. Everything had tons of sugar in it. We were the original little adrenaline junkies. We didn't have helmets, leathers, or knee pads, but we were going for it!

At that point, looking into the house and seeing the motorcycle, we had to have it. So, we used our ingenuity, and Dan's Christmas present, which was a little home welder kit, to cut the lock on the fence and break into the house. Once we were in, I started the motorcycle inside the house and rode it down the back stairs. Did I mention we were little maniacs?

We took it dirt bike riding to where they were building the new housing tracks and were catching massive air. We couldn't wait to really be like Evel Knievel. No more peddling. It was all throttle and air at that point and we were having a great time, not thinking about the consequences to come!

The following week, the owner of the motorcycle started banging on the neighborhood doors asking the parents if they had seen a stolen motorcycle. Well, they hadn't actually seen it, but it could be heard in the distance throughout the day, like a chain saw. Naturally, they asked us if we had seen it. We had hid it in the back of Dan's house in the chicken coup until we could see who the guy was. We went to meet him and were mortified. It was full contact karate champ, real life, badass Bob Wall, aka O'Hara from the movie *Enter the Dragon*! What are the odds of that? Scary. "What?! He's going to kill us!" we said. He offered a huge reward to anyone who could give him info leading to his motorcycle.

It was extremely valuable. This motorcycle had belonged to none other than the biggest A list star, Steve McQueen, the King of Cool, as he was known. I knew I had seen that bike before. In the movie *The Great Escape* he jumped a motorcycle, doing the stunt himself. And here we were riding that motorcycle around like it was some cheap Honda! It should have been in a museum. Bob wanted blood. Ours!

Bruce Lee and Bob Wall were martial arts instructors to Steve McQueen, Kareem Abdul Jabbar, James Coburn, and many other famous Hollywood people. This is not the way we wanted to meet him. I'll never forget one of the last times I would ever talk to Dave. When he met Bob, he was such a Bruce Lee fan that instead of saying, "It's a pleasure to meet you, Sir," he said, "You looked kind of stiff in the movie compared to Bruce Lee." This was coming from a 12-year-old kid and we were just about to talk to Bob Wall. He looked at Dave, pulled back his hand, and said, "You little shit! Who the hell are you?! You don't even know what you're talking about. Bruce Lee was my friend. I don't need to explain anything to you. Get the hell away from me and don't ever come near me again, you punk ass." Wow! Not a good time for us to talk to Bob about the bike!

"What's next? How do we collect the reward money, be friends with Bob, give the bike back; not get in trouble, but get the money too?" We actually said that to each other, not realizing how stupid it was, and how ahead of us Bob was. He didn't care about giving anybody reward money. He knew that whoever knew about the bike was guilty.

We were sick and nauseated for about a week. We didn't know what to do, until Dan's parents found the motorcycle in the chicken coup. Oh...looks like we are clucked now! It all came out. Bob wasn't too understanding at the time, and for a while, we had to do work around his house as a punishment and get slapped around during that time. We had to take it, and it was called karate lessons. Thank God the world wasn't politically correct during those days. But it was worth it. Besides, Bob was the kind of guy that would have kicked our parents' ass if they would have said anything to him. Bob, if you're out there, you are a great friend and an idol to me. Sorry about the bike. Thanks for the life lessons. Personally, I think you looked great in *Enter the Dragon*!

The reward was unbelievable. On any given Sunday, we would play volleyball in Bob's back yard and we had seen everyone from Chuck Norris, Benny "The Jet" Urquidez, Mike Stone and Ed Parker, to Judo Gene Lebell. These guys were the heavy weights of full contact karate; the Pioneers; the Badasses; the guys that were on cover of *Black Belt* magazine every month.

Chuck Norris' action films were just starting to come out at the time. We could have never met Bruce Lee since he had already passed on, but we got to hear all these guys talking about their memories and experiences with him. That's as good as it gets. That was about the time that I started to get influenced by martial arts and stuntmen. I started doing some basic karate because Bob told me, "Get your basics down, and then I will teach you how to fight." It was then that I understood the difference between movie martial arts and being in a real, life-threatening fight. I would soon learn more from the best.

I walked into a dojo in Studio City that said "Ninjutsu". I was always interested in martial arts weapons, from shurikens, nunchucks, katana swords and the famous Japanese Samurai weapons. I met this nut who said he was Frank Dux of the movie *Bloodsport* that Jean-Claude Van Damme starred in.

The story goes like this. Frank Dux's real life was working for Special Ops, the U.S. military and he had studied with a famous Japanese Master. He went on to fight in something called a "Kumite," an underground, full contact, to the death, invitation-only fight in the Hong Kong underworld. I don't know how much of this part is true or what really happened, as not too many people were allowed to witness it. However, I can say by training and being in Dux Ninjutsu dojo, he was one crazy son of a bitch. It was a lot of kill tactics, commando moves, knives, swords and other crazy weapons. He was definitely the real deal, being instructed by world-famous Billy Blanks, and also Marshall Teague, who was the nemesis in the movie *Roadhouse* and the captain in the movie *Armageddon*.

Marshall and I knew each other from 20th Century Fox Studios, where I use to run the commissary and executive dining room. In those days, we had "MASH", "Heart to Heart", "The Love Boat", and "The Fall Guy" all filming at the same time. That's when I jumped ship and started working in the studio system on "Fall Guy" and doing stunts. But that's a story for a later time.

Anyway, after training with Frank for a little while, he moved out of California. So, I moved onto doing some Aikido. I thought it was smooth, and cool to watch, so I wanted to try it. I was training at "Tenshin Dojo," on Santa Monica and La Cienega, with Steven Seagal as the instructor. *Hard to Kill* had just come out and he was starting to become a rising star and couldn't do much class time anymore. Instead, he started doing larger seminars, which I attended at Occidental College; a lot more people showed up. It was good for a while, but he was getting too big in films, and too far away from doing private instruction anymore.

I left there and went on to train with the world's best. I found myself taking occasional lessons with Grand Master Sensei, Gokor Chivichyan. He is Sensei Uncle Gene Lebell's best student. Let's start with Gene Lebell. Gene is known as one of the toughest men alive, and boy I will say, he sure is. Gene is not only an accomplished champion Judo expert, and known as the "Godfather of Grappling," but he was also one of the world's top stuntmen and stunt coordinators. He is also known for fighting the world's first MMA fight in 1963 against Milo Savage.

However, th fight didn't start out that way. There was a reporter, who opened his big mouth about Judo, calling it "all a fraud," and challenging any Judo masters in the world that he would kick their ass boxing. It was Ed Parker that brought the article to Gene, who said he'd take the fight. You gotta know that Gene grew up at the world famous Olympic Auditorium in LA, and ran that place with people and gangsters like Mickey Cohen and boxers like Muhammad Ali, who got his start there. Gene grew up as a kid watching wrestlers and fighters, learning real wrestling moves and judo tips anyone from Ed "Strangler" Lewis to Gorgeous George.

Young Gene would wear a mask on his face and fight the other fighters and wrestlers, either as a stand-in, or as a replacement. So, what do you think happened? He got bad ass. He was also a judo champion, as you will see in the picture below.

Once this guy found out who he was gonna fight, he stuck in a ringer, Milo Savage, ranked as the 5th boxer in the world. When Gene got there to the fight, they even had the nerve to tell him, "You can't do any kicks and can't do any karate chops". Gene held up a book that said judo on it and said, "Can I do anything in this book?" They scrolled through the book and it showed some old black and white step-by-step judo moves. They laughed and said, "Yeah sure, go ahead." Aha! The joke was on them. They picked the wrong guy!

When Gene showed up for the fight that was supposed to be against the reporter, he realized they had substituted Milo Savage. Gene obliges. "Ok, I'll fight him". What Gene didn't know is that they put Milo Savage in a karate gi and greased it up with Vaseline. To top things off, Savage was supposed to have boxing gloves on. Not only did he *not* have boxing gloves on, he had thin wraps with real brass knuckles underneath. You could see it in the fight, as it ripped through Gene's black belt and karate gi as he was giving body shots!

Regardless, Gene wasn't having it. He bounced Milo around in the ring, as Milo was predicted to knock out Gene in the first round with the first punch. Well, if you went up against Gene with an attitude, he'll give you "an attitude adjustment." And he surely gave him one, opening a can of whoop-ass on Milo Savage. He threw him against the ropes, letting the ropes rebound him, and then he hip-threw him, known as a "Harai Goshi". Gene then landed on his chest, knocked the shit out of him and put him in a sleeper hold. Knocked his ass right out!

He must have tripped on Milo's brass knuckles, because he accidentally stepped on Milo's chest and throat after he won. Whoops. By the end of the fight, everyone thought Gene had literally killed Milo; he was out for 20 minutes. It wasn't until Gene had his trainer go over and revive him by a quick, hard shove up into the diaphragm that Milo started to regain some consciousness. You should really search this fight on YouTube!

It was the world's first MMA victory for judo. Shortly thereafter came grabbling, and later jui jitsu, which would come into play and dominate the World and the UFC. Thank you, Uncle Gene.

Returning to the topic of attitude adjustments, Steven Seagal was once on set with Sensei Gene. Seagal liked his movies to have a lot of realism, so he would use real moves and hurt stuntmen on purpose to make his movies look more realistic. Gene and the rest of the stuntmen didn't appreciate that. One day on the set, Gene was telling his stories like only Gene could, with a crowd gathering around him. I guess Seagal didn't appreciate that, so, he walked over to Gene and said, "Hey. So, you're the world's toughest man huh?" and Gene said, "That's what they tell me." So Seagal asked, "What would you do if I did this?" Gene countered the move quickly with a grappling move and Seagal tried another one. It was at that point that Gene had had enough. He put Seagal in a choke hold. There are two kinds of choke holds: one kind is when you wanna put someone to sleep, and the other kind is when you put them in a what Gene calls "a stretch". This is a painful choke out with the blade of your arm on the front of the throat instead of the "V" of your arm on the two arteries, which would simply and gently put someone to sleep. Gene wanted to hurt him, so he put him in a stretch and then to sleep.

When Seagal woke up, he had to go change his pants. He had soiled himself, as Gene told me. Segal then came back to Gene and said, "You will never work on my set again," in which Gene replied, "That's okay, because your career in Hollywood is finished." At that time, Bob Wall and the rest of the *Black Belt* magazine lynch mob had gotten wind of what happened. They called out Seagal for a full contact fight. All he had to do was pick any of these guys for a real fight. Now, I really don't care how bad ass you are, that's a lot to take on. And here we are yet again with Bob Wall, a friend of Gene's. It was not a good career move where Seagal was concerned.

Nonetheless, I have no hard feelings against Seagal; he taught me some good Aikido. But I chose to continue with the toughest man alive, training with Sensei Gene, and his number one student, Grand Master Sensei Gokor Chivichyan, "The Armenian Assassin." He was by far the baddest man alive and a living legend. And by the way, Sensei Gene actually taught Bruce Lee grappling, judo, and jui jitsu. One of Gene's favorite sayings, as you see on the patch of my jump suit is, "When in doubt, choke them out." And he's not kidding.

I eventually strayed off the path of martial arts for a while and took the Hollywood crack cocaine, crazy stuntman route that led me into dark places. But it was martial arts that helped bring me back. A great friend, and one of the world's best judo and jui jitsu instructors, Sensei Santos Flaniken of Malibu Judo, helped reel me back in. He got me going back to Sensei Gene and Gokor's, later to be known as "Hayastan MMA". In the meantime, they had a dojo in Hollywood. You would find everyone training there, from the likes of Chuck Norris, to Bob Wall, to Benny "The Jet" Urquidez, to top Hollywood stunt coordinators and Sensei Santos himself, and of course the world's best, Gokor, who actually could beat any of the Gracie family or anyone in the jui jitsu and MMA World.

It was Gokor that allowed the blessing of the Gracies dojos to sprout up everywhere. Gokor wanted to stay focused and exclusive. When they first asked him to create a franchise, he said he didn't want a McDonald's type martial arts franchise. Although Gokor has some 40 sub-satellite dojos around the world, he goes and instructs at every one himself to this day. He also teaches Air Marshals, LAPD, Marine Corps and Special Forces some devastating moves in self-defense.

After some time spent at Krav Maga with an Israeli commando named Hezi, I ended up going full-time private instruction with Sensei Gokor, Sensei Gene and Sensei Benny. I got to train with other famous fighters from the UFC as well.

Benny "The Jet's" professional fighting record stands at 200 plus wins and zero losses. His accomplished World Title Defense Record stands at 63 wins and zero losses, with 57 knockouts. Unprecedented in ring history, Benny "The Jet" is the only fighter to have retained six World Championships in five weight divisions for 24 consecutive years. Such an honor to be able to say these guys are my Sensei.

But it is Gokor who not only became a best friend and life mentor, but also family to me. I love what he stands for, the way he instructs and how humble he is. He once took on a Marine Corps Special Forces and National Kickboxing Champion at an exhibition for the Marines. The guy tried to show off in front of the other Marines, so he got an attitude adjustment. Gokor took one specialized downward shin kick onto the Marine's femur and broke his leg on the spot in front of all the Marines.

Another time, Gokor was offered $10,000 to fight a UFC Champion, a Latin guy with a real bad attitude. He turned it down, so they showed up at one of Gokor's seminars. He watched Sensei Gokor instruct, and then got into a judo gi with a white belt on and tried to pull one over on Gokor. In front of a large group, the fight was on. Gokor knew that this was no white belt, and he recognized who the guy was. He got him in the world famous Gokor Arm Bar, later to be taught and made famous by Rhonda Rousey. He told the guy, "Tap out, my friend. I know who you are." The guy told Gokor to fuck off. And in the words of Gokor as he tells a story, he pulled back, pulled on the arm, and "CLACK!...broken shoulder." It was such a bad break that it destroyed the guy's career!

Sensei Gokor had never lost a match in his life. Not only was he a judo champion, but he has beaten Olympic champions; and you're not supposed to know this, but in his early years, he would make money by coaching fighters in unsanctioned fights that were held in warehouses. Sensei Gene would coach the fighter in any style of fighting and put

the money up. But Shhhhh... don't tell anyone. It was the original cage fighting UFC, MMA all or nothing, with no tap outs. The real Blood Sport. OUCH!

Gokor's crowning achievement was against a Japanese fighter named "Mr. Maeda." He was offered, I think, somewhere around 6-figures to fight in every style, from world judo, kickboxing and full contact. This beast of a fighter had run out of contenders to compete against, and nobody in the world wanted to fight him. This was Sensei Gokor's Milo Savage moment. Gokor was doing good in his dojo. He had just gotten together with the most wonderful woman, Noreen Chivichyan, and he also had a gold and jewelry business. So why rock the boat? Because, as I have learned, you don't get to be "The World's Toughest Men" without getting out of your comfort zone. This is why I can see so far, because I stand on the shoulders of Giants.

Gokor had accepted the challenge, but at the time, nobody thought he could win. Maeda stood at 6'3", 225 lbs. and was a monster. You should really look up this fight. You can't tell me Maeda wasn't using any juice or steroids at the time. But Gokor took up the challenge and at 5'10 and 185 lbs., made work out of the giant...pulling him to the ground, jumping into an inverted arm bar and rolling him over, as Maeda grasps his wrists and giant arms together, refusing to yield. Gokor, with maneuvers like a python, stuck his foot and heel in against his arm while pulling his other arm. Defeat was inevitable. As big as Maeda's arms were, Gokor had bound them, using both his arms and legs. Wouldn't you know it, another smart ass who didn't want to tap out. CLACK! Broken shoulder. Gokor is responsible for more broken bones than osteoporosis!

Gokor was also an accomplished stuntman and stunt coordinator. He was actually the fight coordinator for the movie *Blood Sport*. What are the odds of that? I was working with Sensei Gokor when I was filming part of my TV show, "Adrenaline Man," where his choke out saved my life. "Adrenaline Man" is a tribute to the real stuntmen, daredevils and especially the guys in Stunts Unlimited and Stuntmen's Association, like Buddy Joe Hooker, Dar Robinson, Hal Needham…the real fall guys, the Ronnie and Reid (RIP) Rondell Safety Team and Charlie and Chuck Picerni, who I grew up with and knew as some of the best stunt drivers in the world. I got tired of watching all of the candy-ass, green screened, fake wire-work BS in Hollywood these days, so I came up with "Adrenaline Man".

Ten episodes were filmed globally of me doing REAL stunts, just like Evel Knievel and the movie *Hooper;* parachute-less jumps, getting shot out of a cannon from a 500-foot bridge, diving outside of the into great white shark infested waters and being lit on fire for the world's record! However, regardless of my adrenaline junkie days, to think that I could beat Gokor when it came time to our fight in the Octagon would have been complete BS. He put me in a sleeper, which I was all too familiar with.

Early on, Sensei Gene had put me in front of the news cameras as ABC filmed it. One person was hand selected by Gokor, and out of about 60 of us there, I was sitting closest to the camera and was somehow volunteered. Sensei Gene is a joker at best. He was putting me in a sleeper and explaining to the media what he was doing to me. I was trying to tap out on his arm and the last thing I remember was Sensei Gene saying to the camera operators, "What Andre is attempting to indicate, while he is hitting my shoulder, is that he has had enough. And that's known as a tap ooooouut." Lights out! That's all I remember. By the time I woke up, the news crews were gone and the shot was finished.

In the picture below, you'll witness Gokor putting me in a full sleeper choke out. My camera man informed me, "You can just shut your eyes and fake it." I replied, "No. Adrenaline Man does the real deal stunts." When he proceeded to put me under, my eyes rolled back and I started to go into what looked like a seizure. You couldn't have faked that or acted that out, even if you were Russell Crowe. It was priceless. But hey, you gotta come out of your comfort zone. It was after that, that Sensei Gokor had respect for me and decided to take me on for private instruction, which he wasn't willing to do prior to the shoot.

 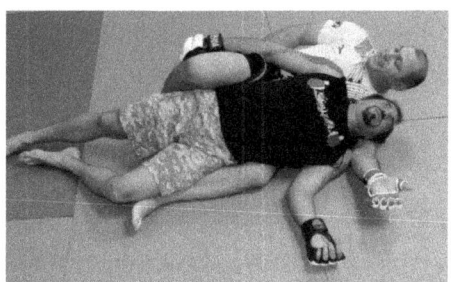

Once I had regained consciousness, Gokor asked me, "Did you see the dream, my friend?" You see, when some people are put in a choke hold or sleeper, they have a dream, and the case was no different for me. My dream was that I was on the ground at a party had just peed all over myself; everyone was standing around pointing at me. So, I said, "No. But I see that the nightmare is still over me." Sensei Gene, after he would put you in a sleeper, would pour warm water on your groin area so when you woke up, you thought you peed on yourself. And I was concerned about that, so it was my concern, even in the subconscious state of being. Alright, never mind the Freudian slip. Let's move on!

Gokor had been doing the choke outs on me on a regular basis. I was trying to build up a resistance and was getting a little better on my time. What was the point? I wanted to calculate exactly what I would see, and how many seconds I had, before I went under. Even some of his top UFC fighters wouldn't allow him to do this to them. And trust me when I tell you, it's very scary. If someone ever does choke you out, you are done... and lifeless. They can do anything to you after that! Makes you think.

It was around that time that I was skydiving with my wife Lina, who's call sign, by the way, is "Falcon;" She is amazing and has done more jumps than me. Lina was also training with Gokor and me in MMA, as well as in surfing, skydiving and weapons. Without a doubt, she is my training partner, best friend and the love of my life!

It was a Saturday afternoon, the day after training MMA with Gokor and Lina. I had always wondered what it would be like, and after what number of skydives, to have a full parachute malfunction, and if I would live through it. It was driving me crazy not knowing. Every jump I would be thinking obsessively, "Will it be this time?" That day, I was using a borrowed rig to save money and I had a major line twist with this parachute during my jump. That means, upon deploying the parachute, the parachute spins around and twists the line, which does not allow the canopy to fully inflate. As a skydiver, to combat that, you are supposed to kick like a bicycle in the opposite direction while spreading the lines apart over your head. However, if you spend too much time trying to untangle a line, you can go into a flat vertical spin and the G forces will cause you to pass out! Lina was under the canopy, watching me in the air while I was kicking out of a line twist. I counted seven times around. Whew.! Made it out, all the while losing altitude the whole time!

We were scheduled to jump the next day and Lina was feeling tired in the middle of the day, which was unlike her. I told her to go turn on the air conditioning in the car and take a nap. Coincidence would have it that my very next jump out of that plane would be the one that I was anticipating. I just knew for a fact as soon as I pulled for the parachute to deploy, and I heard, "This is it." I had been practicing a new malfunction procedure, which was to hook each hand on each handle simultaneously, first pulling on the cutaway on your right side, waiting a full second, and then pull the reserve.

Many people make the mistake of panicking and pull at the same time. What you are doing there is pulling your reserve into your tangled main. Once you do that , you're done! The other mistake many people die from is that they put both hands on the cutaway side, pull on the cord, and as soon as they cut away their main chute, they go for a brand new free fall, which is disorienting. It freaks them out and they can't find the reserve handle to pull in time.

This malfunction was the worst line twist I had ever had. It completely collapsed my canopy to one side, putting me in a vertical spin. I was looking up in the sky and I saw the sparks in the corner of my eyes...the same ones I saw when Gokor choked me out the day before. The G forces were about to choke me out and put me under. I had one second to react. I cut away my main, tried to hang on, and pulled my reserve a second later. Thank God my reserve canopy completely opened. Well that was all great, except now, I'm riding a tiny reserve canopy that I'm not used to!

It was like going from a Cadillac to a little ninja motorcycle. I wasn't ready to switch vehicles, yet I had to figure a way to handle it. Now, take into consideration that the weekend before that, a veteran skydiver, experienced at swooping, inadvertently taught me some things about malfunctions; he had a malfunction at a low altitude, and even with his thousands of jumps prior, ended up in the farmlands and in the weeds. He landed hard and broke his leg, and it took him two hours to drag his ass back to the drop zone, where they finally put him in the car.

So now, I'm hauling ass towards the earth under a canopy, thinking, if the swoop master broke his leg, what can I expect? A new hip? But from training around Mirko, Gokor, Gene and Lina, I had to pull this one off. And by the grace of God, I did.

Not only did I land in the Drop Zone, but I landed right next to my accuracy spot pole, which I was trying to land near with a full-sized canopy. I came in for a great stand up landing. The driver who picks you up drove over to me and said, "I saw the whole thing. Good job. Here's your main canopy." That never happens. Usually you have to scour the farmlands for hours to find your main, if you're lucky and saw the direction it went. I bought the driver two cold beers.

I have mended compound fractures on the drop zone myself, along with Lieutenant Colonel Mirko Djordjevic aka "Soko", who is my skydiving instructor. The Gokor of the air, if you will. Mirko is the world's best combat military instructor, and the world champion formation instructor and personal skydive instructor. Period. Not only that, he is the world's best aerial photographer, always making me look so good in those pictures. In order to get those shots, somebody has to jump backwards and upside down to get me and the bottom of the plane. It's a lot harder than what I do.

It was Mirko that had jumped with me and overheard another jumper regarding my jump. "I knew that was a malfunction when I saw the chute open."

After landing, Mirko ran over to me, gave me a big hug and said he was really proud of what he had taught me and how I handled myself. He went and woke up Lina, saying to her in Serbian accent, "You left him here a boy, but he has returned back a man." She didn't know what he was talking about until he explained my cut away malfunction and what happened. Ever since that day, I have never been obsessive or too concerned about canopy malfunctions. Thank God!

CHAPTER 9

DEATH, DRUGS, DESTRUCTION AND DELIVERANCE

I STILL HAVE A HARD TIME forgiving myself for the death of my best friend Patrick. Patrick was a young actor who featured in the surf movie *Big Wednesday*. We had some amazing times together. We would get up early, around 4:30-5AM, and be dawn patrol. Dawn patrol means you are the first ones in the water as the sun rises. It's a sensational feeling. The winds were calm, slight offshore, and the sets would start rolling in at Malibu 3rd point. We were living the California dream surfer lifestyle.

When I was surfing Malibu 3rd point early in the morning, and it was just too good to pass up, I wouldn't make it to school. Whenever I would go to school, I would come back and surf at the end of the day. The answer was obvious for why I got into continuation and had to do another year of high school? Life was too good and I didn't want to grow up. I had a silver surfer van, all carpeted inside with an 8-track stereo, no windows, brown velour curtains and paneling on the wall. It was like a rolling party room.

I had sun bleached blond hair from surfing twice a day. I completely healthy, aside from the four-foot bong I had in my van, that was so long, that I couldn't even reach the end of; someone always had to light it for me. Back then, we made our own bongs; cut a piece of bamboo, cut another small piece for a stem, and use a thimble from sewing to drill holes in it and you'd have an awesome bowl. We would get baked, paddle out and surf like rock stars, thinking we owned the world.

If we weren't surfing, we were shredding. There was a drought in the San Fernando Valley with plenty houses for sale with empty pools. Me, Patrick and the boys from Dog Town would find these pools and shred on a regular basis.

It was an awesome time to be a teen in the late 70s. I'll never forget going to prom with my custom van and prom tux. I would use the tux later to skate the empty bowls (pools). We also had a place called Skatercross. It was the San Fernando Valley's first skateboard park. *Skateboarder* magazine would come out and look for guys that were really good and hold photoshoots. I got into a couple of them and was heavily influenced by the Z-Boys, and Tony Maddog Alva in particular, as they were dominating skateboarder magazine in bowl riding. Much respect to Z-Boys and Dog Town. But back to the surfing days.

Patrick was a real cool guy. Everyone liked him, including the girls. He was just coming off of *Big Wednesday* and had helped me get my first commercial and stunt job with Mattel. The shot was taken at Sepulveda Dam, where the director wanted me to go up the huge dam embankment,

ride it and do kick turns. So, I did. I rode it like a wave, like it was a swimming pool bowl.

My introduction to Hollywood came when the director yelled "Cut!" I asked him what I had done wrong and he said, "Nothing, but we are trying to sell these *roller skates* from Mattel and you're making them look bad because the roller skater can't keep up with you." I said, "You should be selling Mattel *skate boards* then." Not the first or the last time a director stopped me from doing something so well. But thanks to Patrick, I got my start.

Patrick and I were heading into our late teens and early twenties. We went from long blond hair, to cropped haircuts, and found ourselves going from listening to Led Zeppelin on our way to the beach, to listening to B-52s, Devo, and the Clash. We were drinking 151 and coke in the car and going to new wave and punk rock clubs. I went from early in the morning and healthy, to late night and hammered in Hollywood. Wow! What happened?

The party started getting ugly, but we were having a good time. Patrick's mom got married to a good man named Bob, and Patrick even took his last name; he didn't really like his biological dad. I can relate to that. Then Patrick was starting to slide into a deep depression. He just couldn't find his groove of where he should be. His mom was moving to

Paso Robles, California, which is nothing but ranch land, and Patrick was in Woodland Hills with his future ahead of him. He would have had to stay in Hollywood to work on auditions.

One night, we were smoking some pot in the car and something urged that I should keep my cash hidden underneath my mat, so I did. As we were walking back to the club through an alley in Hollywood, a car pulled up, slammed on its brakes and out climbed two black guys with hand guns. In the diver seat was an older black guy, yelling out orders. We were being robbed. "Give us all your money mother fuckers!" Well, I only had 3 bucks on me and a bottle of red wine that I had just opened. So, I gave them the $3. I stayed calm, or drunk...I don't recall which one it was. They jacked Pat for $25 and were mad that we didn't have more money. My other friend Keith was walking towards us from a distance.

On a tangent note, Keith, just minutes before that, was kissing what he thought was a girl inside of a Hollywood night club. Just as he thought things were going so smoothly, I grabbed him by the back of his shirt and pulled him away. I said "Dude! That's a dude!" He said, "No way," and was mad at me till he sobered up for a second and I told him to look at the hands, the Adam's apple and the large feet. So, he needed to go out and get some air. But back to my story.

The guys who were robbing us were high on crack. The older guy was yelling at them, trying to teach them how to rob people, so they were looking at him going, "$3? We got some wine!" He said, "Dammit just take it." At that point, I realized that I had a shaky gun to my ribcage. I pointed in Keith's direction and said, "I think that guy has some more money for you." I figured if Keith was dumb enough to kiss a dude he thought was a girl, he should pay a little bit for it. So, I put these guys onto Keith and split. I know it sounds bad, but I thought it was funny at the time.

I ran back inside the club. Didn't think much of it until my friends came back in. They thought they were going to call the police, but the manager said, "This is Hollywood. That happens all the time." Now the strange part about that is that the nightclub belonged to Eddie Nash, of the infamous Laurel Canyon murders. The name of the club was called Seven Seas, and it was right across the street from Grauman's Chinese Theatre. You could tell it was an old Hollywood drinking bar that was used in the 40s by our military because it was so old and everything was "tikied" out. There were tiki lights, tiki torches, tiki bamboo…just a real old South Pacific wanna-be Waikiki bar turned into a new wave night club.

Ironically, across the street at Grauman's Chinese Theatre was where I used to walk around as a little kid. Now, I'm over here on the dark side of the boulevard with the crackheads, getting robbed. Welcome to Hollywood. I guess all roads cross somewhere in life. Mine had once I met a girl named Teri Peterson, who won the Miss Sunkissed Malibu bikini contest and got a deal with *Playboy* to be Miss July. I was seeing her around that time, and the bad part about it was that she went from being the healthiest girl on the beach, to becoming a model.

What does being a model in Hollywood mean? It meant you started snorting coke, dating an older loser German photographer and getting hooked on heroin. It was sad to see, but I was drowning in my own world. The first try happened the night we went to prom; it was popular to snort some cocaine. We were pretty innocent about it, at first. It started out with a quarter gram to a gram, making tiny lines and having a little champagne to wash it all down. It later turned into doing massive rails, one gram each line and it really started to mess me up.

I never got into heroin, having had a near death scare. I went over to Teri's place on Melrose and brought some coke. We did a few lines and a group said, "We need to go to the store. We'll be right back." While they ran a store errand to get alcohol, I went into the kitchen and saw a gram of cocaine. I had run out, so I did what anybody would do when they run out of cocaine- snort someone else's. I had a pocket full of cash and figured, "What the heck, I'll reimburse them when they get back." So, I snorted it and feeling nothing. Huh! Must be junk or cut.

They came back, went to the kitchen and walked back out. They asked, "Andre! What happened to that pile in the kitchen?" I said, "I snorted it. Here's the money." They were shocked. They said, "You need to sit down. You just snorted the largest amount of China White *heroin* we have seen anybody do." I was in trouble!

They stuck me in the corner, put in some jazz, gave me a bowl of ice cream and just monitored me for a few hours. I started nodding in and out of consciousness. Once I had thrown up, the buzz really began to kick in. If you don't know, most people who do heroin tend to throw up. It was sad to see Teri go from being beautiful and healthy to me holding her hair on the side of some building while she was yacking. And it gets worse.

I finally made it through that night and made my way home. I was high for almost three days, and the scary part was that I liked it. But I knew that if I ever got into heroin and sticking needles in my arm, that it'd be over. So, I just stuck with snorting coke, and kept snorting coke until some idiots somewhere said, "Hey! Our heart's not blowing up fast enough snorting it…let's smoke rock!" For all of you that don't know what that is, its crack cocaine, or freebasing, and had begun to get to epidemic proportions in LA. So for me, since I liked snorting coke and smoking pot, I figured, why not smoke coke? What an idiot!

Coke had a deep tradition in Hollywood. Even back in the day, if you watched black and white movies, there were references to it. Jean Harlow would call certain girls in her movies "snow birds," which were what we call our modern day "coke whores". Snow birds were girls that would hang around the Hollywood scene to get high on cocaine and be around entertainment industry people. Not much has changed. In Hollywood on Sunset Blvd in the 20s, after working long hours in the studio, you could actually go into bars on Sunset (now the Sunset Strip) and on the bar top would be little crystal bowls with cocaine in them. Crazy, huh? But part of Hollywood.

Somebody once said to me, "Cocaine is God's way of telling you that you are making too much money. And if you are spending it on cocaine, it's a waste." And it's true. Later, we would have jokes for our addiction. I don't like cocaine, I just like the smell of it. Nonetheless, I started smoking it and the party went from the beach, to the Hollywood night clubs, to crack motels. Really bad.

But let's return to Patrick for a minute. Patrick was heavily depressed and had begun to slit his wrists. I hadn't noticed at the time since he wore long sleeves. One day he said, "I saw a TV special on suicide. Do you die right away if you shoot yourself in the head?" Since I knew guns, he had asked me, and I said, "Oh no. No. No." I had known the answer to that first hand.

When my mom and dad came to America after the war, they had a couple of best friends who were very poor and lived in Pasadena. I remember as a kid going to their house and some of the rooms actually had dirt flooring, as in real dirt as the floor. One day, the husband, Milan, said to my dad. "I got a tip on an investment for a company. You need to go in on this with me."

My dad said with pride, "Oh no. I went to University. I have my career." Even though they were struggling too, Milan's investment paid off massively. He's a billionaire now and owns one of the largest pharmaceutical companies in the world. Just overnight, he had become extremely wealthy. But with wealth, comes great temptation and sin.

After that, my mom and dad never talked to them anymore. I asked them why. They said, "Because everyone is all up on them for money and we don't wanna be that way." I said, "But you were best friends!" And they replied that money changes people. The man had become so wealthy, he figured he'd have a girl or two on the side, putting up a girl in his condo at Newport Beach. But his wife also had money, so she hired a private detective and found out about a girl.

She called the girl's house and she answered. The wife demanded, "Let me speak to my husband." They were both kind of shocked and surprised. The husband got on the phone and said, "I'll explain everything later." She said, "Tell me you love me. Now. Out loud in front of her." And he replied, "We will talk about this later. We will discuss it later and I will explain." She told him again, "Tell me you love me in front of her." He wouldn't. And they both heard "BANG!" on the other end of the phone. She had shot herself in the head!

She didn't die right away. She lived like a vegetable for a few months, but even all of his money couldn't rescue her. Years later, his sin caught up with him again through his son, on the day of his graduation from his expensive school in Switzerland. You see, you have to send your kid away when you're responsible for their mom's death due to your own sins. His son, the heir to his throne and fortune, had partied at a Barcelona hotel. The hotel had very low steel railings and he fell over, plummeting down the court yard, and splitting his head open on his graduation night. The father's sin had been catching up with him and his life as if he was cursed.

After I told Patrick this story I said, "The best way is a shot to the heart, it's over." I later received a chilling phone call from Patrick's mom, telling me that Patrick had shot himself in the wine cellar, through the heart. He had been slipping on depressants and alcohol and it never occurred to me that when I was instructing him on how one could effectively commit suicide, he was the one trying to kill himself.

I am still struggling with forgiving myself for giving him that info. RIP Patrick Beckwith, my dear friend. After his passing, we went out on a huge sailboat to Rincon Point in Ventura County, and I was at the bow dumping his ashes into the water. I would later be doing the same thing from a helicopter in Arizona for the man who became my real dad…Rae Williams.

After Patrick passed, another best friend of mine, Wayne, had gotten into a car accident and got way too much money for it. It was an excessive amount of money for a young guy who liked to smoke cocaine. One day he was at my house with a sketchy, greasy, little guy named Chip. Chip was the kind of guy that you hated right when you met him. He was wiry and untrustworthy at best. I remember we were getting high and Chip said something stupid. I told Wayne that I was going to take him outside and beat the shit out of him, which is something everyone wanted to do when they met Chip.

Wayne told me that Chip had just gotten out of prison. He was a little older than us (but looked younger) and that if I were to do that, Chip was the kind of guy that would wait behind a bush, a building, or a car, and literally stab you in the back with a knife sooner or later. He said, "It's not worth it, Andre." I said, "Wayne, get him out of here." And he did.

Well, not too shortly after that, I got a chilling phone call. You see, Wayne had been partying with Chip and probably couldn't take much more. They were smoking coke, and maybe they ran out, or it was the last hit, I don't know. But it was in Calabasas, California…the night Chip murdered Wayne. Chip had attacked him from behind, violently stabbing him many times. Wayne had managed to get out of the door and out to the other condos. Bloody, and on the verge of death, he desperately pounded on doors for help!

Apparently, no one would open the door to help him. Running out of blood, Wayne eventually collapsed against a wall, bleeding to death. As the paramedics arrived, a crowd of people formed; the same people that wouldn't help Wayne. With his last dying breath, he looked up at all the people staring down at him and said, "I can't believe you all let me die." So here I am, finding out that we aren't immortal, don't own the world and don't live forever!

I had later found that most of the friends I had grown up with were either gone, addicted to drugs or dead. So, I kept moving on, just hanging and banging away. The crack had gripped the city of LA.

One night, after watching a Chuck Norris movie, I went with a friend into a Vons market in North Hollywood at 1:30AM. We had gotten what we needed and started to walk back to the front of the store when I said, "Hold on. I forgot to get a can of dog food." Just as I turned around and went back down the aisle, I heard male voices shouting and screaming at the cashier and box boy. They had guns on them and were demanding money. They were high, sketchy and shaky.

As I peeked around the corner, a guy with a 1911 smoked the box boy, hitting the poor kid with a .45 round to the chest. The round picked him off the ground and put him back four feet! The 1911 .45 round was developed to be a body stopper during the South Pacific wars. The Japs would pump themselves up full of opium and wrap themselves with tight linen so even if you shot them with your service rifle, they'd keep coming at you with a huge bayonet. In short, the job of the 1911 .45 was to hit you so hard that it would actually push you back. But when used on an unarmed human being, it's a brutal thing to see.

Those were the kinds of times in LA we were living in. Guys, and gangs like these, were taking the cashiers and customers into the back of the market, to the meat locker where no one would hear them, brutally gang raping girls and killing the rest. I knew that I had to do something fast. This guy was lying on the ground bleeding to death. I had a girl with me that I was concerned for, plus here comes an elderly couple down the aisle. What to do?

I did what Chuck Norris would do. I took the big can of dog food I had with me and threw it as hard as I could two or three isles over, making a crashing sound. I figured that would solve it, but it didn't. Now these guys came looking for us. I ran everyone to the back of the market and we hid behind the display case. I remember saying, "Please God, what do I do?" and a still, small voice told me, "Turn around." I saw a door to the back of the market that said in big red letters "EMERGENCY DOOR. ALARM WILL SOUND IF OPENED." I took a running start at that door. I felt like I must have done a Bruce Lee kick, sound effects and all, into that door and it burst open, smashed against the wall and the alarm went off in the whole market.

I got the people out of the back door. I didn't know if the thugs had left the building or not, but I was pretty sure if you're sketched and cracked out, hearing alarms is not where you wanna stay. I ran up to the front and use my shirt and fingers to plug the hole in the guy that got shot. I was talking to him, but he was in complete shock. If you'd ever see a fish trying to breath out of water, you can imagine what he looked like. By the time the paramedics arrives, he was still barely alive, and they took him out of there.

I made a follow-up phone call the next day to check on him. The hospital said he was in critical condition. I wish I had been further in my walk with God to go visit him and pray for him, but I wasn't, so I didn't. This started to become almost normal for me...seeing shootings and stuff. I was becoming numb to it. Sometimes I would be carrying weapons too. It was just a part of living in the "City of Angels". What kind of angels? Can't be good ones!

But, I have had some good angels save my hide many times. There must be a dispatch room in Heaven with God sending out angels to work overtime just for my sorry ass. Because whether trouble found me, or I found trouble, I was a magnet for that shit.

After my tour of strip clubs, I am ashamed to say, I would hang out with biker gangs. A friend of mine that I played high school football with, he was fullback, was also into full contact kick boxing; I also knew his younger brother. He was always wide and thick built, so it was befitting that had the words "President of the Hell's Angels" and his chapter tattooed onto his back. So, I had my share of friends in the H.A.s at the time.

I had been asked to be a prospect since I rode Harleys. But thank God I had the sense to pass on that. One way in. No way out. I respect them and understand them, but don't hang out with them anymore. I later started hanging out with a crazier bunch, Special Ops, SEAL teams and Marine Corps.

In case you all didn't know how the Hell's Angels got started, the Hell's Angels were badass fighter pilots from WWII. After flying around in P-51 Mustangs, bombing and killing (well deserved) Nazis, they came back to America with the need for speed. They started chopping motorcycles, making them light and faster and speeding around the U.S.A., chasing the adrenaline rush. There's more to the story than this, but it's not my story to tell.

One night, I'm standing at another bar when a little Latin gangster named Rudy went off on this big white guy. The big white guy was younger and kind of dumbfounded, and Rudy had anger management issues. He was known to be a maniac, but we finally talked him off the ledge, telling him to go outside and cool off. He kicked the door open and said, "You want me to go outside?! I'll frickin' go outside!" Good, we thought.

Well, he went outside alright, but he came back inside with something on his side. Oh, here we go, another hand gun. By now, I had become accustomed to seeing them, but this time he had it pointed two feet away to the chest of this white guy. Rudy really respected me. My guess was that it was because I wasn't stupid or too fearful of stuff. Without even thinking, I stepped in between the gun and the white guy. Yeah, I know. It was a dumb thing to do! But I felt like I had to do it. Rudy had pulled the hammer back and was about to "blast a fool", as they say in the hood. But for whatever reason, I didn't think he would blast me. So, I stepped in between and calmly said, "Rudy! Rudy! He's not worth it. You are going to go back to prison if you do this. Calm down. You're about to get married." His girlfriend was crying, and everyone else was silent. I remember looking at his eyes, his eyebrows furrowed in an angry rage. Everything seemed to move in slow motion at that point and nobody knew what he was going to do. He exhaled with his teeth gridded and lowered the gun. Thank God! I was running out of shirts to plug peoples' holes with, especially if it was my own!

I had seen an overwhelming amount of violence from my days in jail or cracked out on the streets in Inglewood, Compton, and downtown LA. But this incident was completely unexpected occurring in a place called Sagebrush Cantina in Calabasas, California. It was a Sunday evening at the end of a Memorial Day weekend, and hundreds of Harleys, riders, biker gangs, porn stars, wanna-be's and other assorted nuts would show up to drink margaritas and tequila in the warm sun. Motorcycle gangs and people don't mix, and it was that afternoon that I ran into a guy named Angie Reno.

Angie was one of the toughest guys out in Malibu Surf Break. Now, I know what you are all envisioning. Warm water, beautiful waves, and hundreds of blond haired guys all spiritually surfing together in a peaceful Zen environment. Bullshit! There's boards banging, colliding with each other and people screaming and yelling, "My wave!" There was even a guy who put a pair of opened scissors onto the front of his board with resin, just in case someone took off in front of him. It was an alpha male, primal pack mentality. You either better know how to shred, or better know how to get out of the way, because three or four guys dropping in on a 15-foot wave coming right at you with a pointy fiberglass projectile at eye level would sober you up real quick. I got 12 stitches right next to my eye to prove it. My friend Mike got 150 stitches in his head after having his scalp peeled back by a moron on a long board that was going left on a right point in Malibu, and didn't know what he was doing. There are thousands of stupid stories like this from Malibu. If you don't know what you are doing, stay out of the lineup!

It was a common occurrence to see guys go out onto the beach and duke it out over a stupid wave; it happened all the time. It even got to the point where we perfected an art form of fighting in the water so you didn't lose any waves or time. You would paddle up next to the guy, sit up on your board and just dive onto him. With your left hand out, you grab him by the front of his hair and pull him under water, and when he comes up for a breath, you hammer fist him in the nose three or four times. That way, you drown with a little of your own blood. It was brutal. But that's how it was at Malibu 3rd point on big summer swells. Everyone and their brother who hadn't surfed for most of the year decided, "Now's the time to come out," and you could tell. I usually knew most of the surfers, so I was okay as part of the pack and had no problem calling anyone onto the beach. And that's just how you had to be. It's a stupid male mentality!

Angie was known for pulling people out of the water and beating the shit out of people in record time. He also lived in a house next to Malibu Pier, so he owned those waters along with great surfers like Dave White and Johnny Gyro. Dave was little, but he would fight anybody, any size, anytime. And he was as good at fighting as he was at surfing. There were other regulars, such as Allen Sarlo of Dog Town Z-Boys and Zuma Jay aka Jefferson Wagner of the movie *Arms Management*, who I got to work with as an armorer, doing weapons and stunts. They were no one to be messed with. But some guys were just so good, and so respected for their surfing skills, that others would just get out of their way, such as my board shaper and dear friend Glen Kennedy of Kennedy Surf Boards.

As for Johnny Gyro, he got that nickname because he was known for shredding up and down the wave in a gyrating motion. His real name was John Potter. Boring huh? Johnny had long blond hair almost to his waist, wore a bright yellow wetsuit and had a big mouth. You would always hear and see him coming. People didn't like him because he was loud, so Johnny started taking karate seriously. He got into a fight with three military guys at the Pizza Hut in Malibu and beat the shit out of all of them at one time. He got a reputation after that. No to mention, Johnny hung out with Dave all the time. So, if you fought one, you fought both. But it usually wouldn't come to that, because one was all you would be able to handle.

Later, Johnny took his nickname, Johnny Gyro, to full contact karate tournaments and is now known for his amazingly fast spinning kicks. I am proud to say he's a great friend, like an older brother to me, and owns the extremely successful Johnny Gyro Karate Schools. His schools are known for turning out younger black belt students than most places.

Back to that night. Angie and I were sitting on the corner of the Cantina. I had always wanted to hang out with Angie, but he was so in-character or intimidating at Malibu, that I never got to really talk to him. So, it was an honor to have a drink with him that night and talk about our old times in Malibu. He was a stuntman too and stunt driver on *The Dukes of Hazzard* TV show. He would jump the orange Dodge Charger, known as the "General Lee," with the lovely Confederate Flag on it. And to all that think it's politically incorrect, I say with all do disrespect, shut up, stupid!

I have great love for the Confederate flag and the men who fought and died for the freedom of others and slavery. I also love the show Dukes of Hazzard and can't talk about it without talking about my friend, John Schneider, who was one of the Duke Boys. I lived next door to him for a while and had a chance to buy a replica General Lee from his company (that manufactured the replicas), as the originals were all crashed on set, and if there was an original, John would have owned it. They are hard to find, but worth it for what it represents, the V8 muscle car catching massive air. I'm still looking for one, so if anyone's got one for sale, let me know.

It was then that I noticed four or five Vagos biker gang members. You always know the Vagos for their bright green bandana and colors. Although they're not the Hell's Angels, they were no one to be trifled with; some biker gangs have more to prove and are extremely violent. In addition, sometimes they would subcontract work from H.A.s or other gangs so you never knew. In other words, even though my friend was the President of the H.A. you just don't throw that around...and hope you don't need it, because by the time whatever is done to you, it isn't worth it.

Feeling a little uncomfortable around them, I got up for a minute. They all had full leathers on their bandanas, and knives on their side. And I don't mean fold out little knives, I'm talking real hunting knives on their hip. They were starting to get loud and crazy, but unless somebody's in your front yard and you're facing a life-threatening situation, leave it alone and just walk away. Nobody ever truly wins a fight, because even if you win, you still lose for being in one. But still, protect yourself at all cost!

I was in the bathroom when I started to hear shouting and screaming. I ran out to find four or five guys on top of Angie Reno. By the time I could run over to where he was (the Cantina is a big place), they had already ran out the door and were getting on their bikes. Some of you would call this karma for all the guys Angie bloodied up on the beach at Malibu, but his time had come at a Calabasas bar. They had all jumped him, beat on him, and stabbed him multiple times!

As I got to Angie, he was on the floor with blood everywhere. I don't know how much difference I would have made, but I will say this for Angie...he is one tough son of a bitch to be able to take that. So here we go again. I took off my shirt, put it on the open wound and held him by his side and gut, hoping nothing was going to come out. Coincidentally, I remembered that there was a little Emergency Room across the street.

They even said in the ER, "The Cantina sure sends a lot of business our way". I stayed there while they worked on Angie. When I asked him if he had anyone he wanted me to call for him, he said no. I guess all those years of being the guy with a bad attitude left him with few people that cared. Or maybe he just didn't want anyone to know he got stabbed. Either way, I actually felt sorry for him. It was like seeing a lion in Africa that is attacked by the younger male lions, bloodied up and chased off. He was once the king of the jungle… and look at him now. That's life. Much respect to you Angie; you are one of a kind.

After all the extreme stuff that I'd been doing, from skating empty pools and surfing big waves, to doing stunts and being various near-death experiences, it wasn't enough just to pride myself on being able to outdrink anybody (which by the way is stupid and I'm not encouraging it). After getting drunk I could easily be triggered and fell into deep addiction.

There were plenty of times when we couldn't snort any more coke because our noses were so packed. When we would be doing lines, after two days of snorting, the stuff would fall out of your nose and back onto the mirror. As a result, I turned into a crack head. It was a rush for me at the time, being able to take a huge hit and get so high so quick…it was addictive. The average amount of dopamine in your brain would give you one drip per activity, getting you high and feeling great. But when you took a hit of crack, it was like someone dumped a bucket of dopamine over you. It was just so overwhelming, and so scary, because when you hear the expression, "someone has demons," the meaning was all too real.

I would take a hit, and we called it the "helicopter effect." You'd get so high you'd hear a helicopter in a warehouse echoing in your head. By the way, one is too many and a thousand is never enough with crack. I'd be by myself in crack motels and when I took a hit, I would hear thousands of voices start to whisper in my ears at once. They were the voices of demons from another dimension, and I had agreed to the terms of the crack and opened a portal and tunnel to a dark and dangerous world from which some never return!

Be warned that what I am about to write in this chapter is not for the faint hearted. I won't go as far as to tell you not to let your children read it, because maybe somebody will head my cautions and dark experiences, and not go down the dark satanic road that I did. And if you are already there, know that there is a way out and a light at the end of the tunnel.

Crack is also known as crack cocaine, or the devil's dandruff. As comedian Denis Leary once said, "Never smoke something that's named after your butt (crack)." I can't even begin to tell you all the bad things that happened to me, and all the people I saw die and ruined by this drug; that would fill three books. But I'll give you some...enough that you'd never want to go down that road, God willing.

After drinking and smoking on the Sunset Strip or in Hollywood, I found myself with a high tolerance and I still wanted to party. At the time, everything I did, I tried to do to the most extreme, and unfortunately, that included my partying. So, when everyone else would be going home, I'd still be up at somebody's house in the Sunset Hills and then on to crack motels in Hollywood. It was extremely dangerous because you couldn't think clear on this drug. All you knew is that you had to get your hands on more!

I was once in a motel and people were walking in and out of the room as the crack dealer was selling dope. We were all sitting together with our crack pipes, which consisted of a glass pipe and brillo, or Chore Boy, which are copper scrubbing pads for a kitchen sink. It's the only thing that could withstand the intense flame being put on the hard rock of crack cocaine and whatever other cut was in it at the time. We would be so spun and wide-eyed after taking our hits that we would be tweaking and always looking out of the motel room windows. Someone in the room would say, "Get away from that window!" while they were crawling around on the ground, scrubbing to find another hit on the floor. Most of the time, there wasn't any.

You never knew when somebody, with their friends and desperate for crack, would storm the room with guns or knives; and it happened all the time. If people trying to rob us, 5.0 would raid the rooms on a regular basis. But yet through all the stupidity, we had to stay high.

A guy walked in with a public transport RTD bus driver uniform. He took one hit, stood in the middle of the room and got stuck. This happens frequently. Stuck is when you take such a big hit, you are paralyzed and you just stand there in the middle of the room like an idiot, lock-jawed, while everyone is staring at you. And if that's not enough, when you go to tell the stuck person to knock it off, they start freaking out and go "Shhhhh. Shhhh. Police is here! Police is here!" It would fuck your whole high up. After this bus driver came out of it, I said to him, "You must have just gotten off work." He said, "Nope. I'm on my way in," and he was serious. Well that explains all the bus crashing accidents in downtown LA!

Another time I was smoking crack in a motel, there was a pregnant woman in there. It was horrific to watch because she needed crack, but she was about to have the baby any second. We were just trying to stay high and not get stuck, while this poor girl was smoking one crack hit after another, then a cigarette and then another crack hit. Well, she went into labor, and our plan was to get her into the car and drop her off in front of the Emergency Room. Not too smart of a plan. Anyway, I had to get out of there; it was just too much to deal with and it was freaking me out.

I later found out that she had barely made it to the hospital and was alive, but had delivered a crack baby. If you don't know what that is, it's a tiny trembling addicted baby that still has crack in its system from the mom and its shaking because it wants something, like another hit, but it doesn't know where and how to get it. It's the saddest thing you'd ever seen!

I was partying in Inglewood after dropping someone off at the airport in LAX. I found that the rocks of crack were much larger and better deals in Inglewood and Compton, but much more dangerous. That's where I met NY. He was an ex crackhead from New York who moved to LA to sell dope. Seems like the better dealers were ex crack addicts because they sure knew how to work you, and NY was no exception. He had the best boulders around. And he almost paid for it with his life on several occasions.

The last time was right after I met him. A guy had hit him in the face with a shovel and dropped him on the streets of Inglewood, taking $700 cash, but he hadn't found his stash. NY had a gut that overhung his waist line and he would roll up his dope and stick it up in there. Gross huh? But no one ever found it.

From the first chapter in the book, you will remember reading about a guy named NY who was there when I got arrested by S.W.A.T. I agreed the bank heists because he promised to give me cash and crack at the end of the day. Understand that there are no limits to where that shit will take you.

I was with another dealer named "Miami". Apparently, your street name connects with your city of origin, keeping your identity anonymous. This was a very unusual situation for me, but I found myself in it a few times. Since I was white, they kind of trusted me a little bit more (they were both African American). I worked in the music industry and had cash, and they both wanted to get into the music industry and were dope dealers. In some sort of sick way, I found favor among crack dealers that would prolong my agony and my addiction, who to this day, have done me no favors, except to provide content for this book, and to pass on to you the cautioning information.

During the time of my stay with Miami, though he didn't smoke crack anymore, he had lots of customers so he wanted the best. He employed me to drive him around and sample the crack to tell him my opinion. During that time, there was a killer in Hollywood making his way around the crack community and the streets. He had just gotten out of prison for murder and was desperate to get high, not caring if he went back. He bought a filet fishing knife, extra-long and extra sharp, and would find dope dealers, stabbing them in the heart or throat and taking their stash.

We had heard about this killer and that he and his crew were near us, we just didn't know what he looked like.

Miami had me take him to the military surplus store on Hollywood Blvd to get a huge can of mace. I remember him telling me that when he sprays, that it's going to have some sort of a shattering effect in the air so we, too, may not be able to see while the knives were being swung at us, but to make sure that I pick up a chair and smash it in the right direction. I said Ok and sorty of brushed him off since I was high at the time.

We had heard about another attack and killing just a couple of hours after. It had been all the guys we knew well who had been getting murdered. One of the victims was an older guy we called "Pops"; he got it in the heart. There were always new customers on the streets so you couldn't just shut down your business. As a result, we stuck close together, Miami and I.

One night, Miami asked me to run a cup down to the gas station nearby. I wondered why but I ran down, handed the cup to the guy and took the money. Once I had, even though I was in a well-lit area and prepared, a death chill came over me. I went back and told Miami that I didn't like the guy. He said, "You know why? You just met the Grim Reaper. He's the stabber." "What?! Why did you have me go do that?!" He said, "So I could take a good look at him out the window." So the lesson here is, never take a job as a crack or meth taster from a dealer.

One of Miami's regular clients, a nickel and dime guy, somehow came into some money and Miami had figured it out. This guy had partnered up with the Grim Reaper, and in exchange for dope, he would turn over Miami's life and mine. It was a Friday night and we heard a BANG on the door. Friday nights were when all of the dealers re-up, replenishing their stash by buying more, and this guy knew it.

Remember the military mace? I had a custom pool cue in the room that looked like a shotgun case. We knew it was the Grim Reaper with two of his friends. They were standing on the side of the wall with their knives out, and it was go-time. I can't tell you that I wasn't scared, but I was too focused to think about it. I had grabbed a chair and was ready to push the first guy who came into the room right over the railing of the 2nd floor motel.

You come at me with a knife, I'll do whatever I have to. That's a serious thing. At that point, Miami, with his deep, loud voice, said to him, "Go on!! Come on in, motherfuckers!! I got a 12-gauge shot gun, loaded and ready for your ass!" Of course, we didn't, so I took my pool cue box and slid and banged it at the curtain real quick, hoping it would bluff them. And Miami kept screaming, "Bring it!!"

Well, that made them rethink it and they went downstairs. We didn't know where they went, but we were packed up and ready to leave. I turned on the car alarm to my Suburban to draw attention to the parking lot and anyone that was waiting there. Well, that worked too. Knowing how other crackheads think, tweak and get paranoid, I used that as my edge. So, Miami and I hightailed it out of there and went to another motel while they went on to another stabbing spree!

At that point I figured I needed to go home. I had been rolling around in the streets of Hollywood for over a week. I would disappear for weeks at a time. My brake pads had been worn through and were grinding onto the metal, so it was time to get out of there before I rear ended somebody cracked out because of no brakes. Try explaining something like that. I had to first get some sleep before I started hallucinating. I had built up a tolerance for staying up for days but then it would catch up with me and I would either pass out or start hallucinating. Neither one was good.

I had been known to switch to different crack areas. It was in San Fernando Valley that somebody had asked to borrow my car for a drug run. That's never a good idea because they get high and wreck it, or take your car and leave you sitting in a motel room for hours or days. It's not stealing because you handed them the car keys. Once, I let a girl borrow my car and she came back with the whole side of it ground down. She had cut the corner of a post and ruined the whole side of my car. She had a "Oh well, too bad, white boy" attitude about it. Not much you could do. Crack addicts don't have money, so she gave me some crack for it, but that was gone an hour later. It was then that I realized that she was actually a he. It was an African American male posing as a woman and doing things to get crack, if you know what I mean. But everybody knew it wasn't that kind of party…only women for me.

Another time, I was sitting in a motel room and a guy named Rico had a working girl. She went out to get us some dope and money since we had run out, which in her case, meant she went out to turn a trick, performing sex for money. It was unbelievable what happened next. Some guy in a BMW, in town for a convention, picked her up. She went and got a bunch of crack for him and they started to smoke it. He took the hit and then the guy died behind the wheel of the car while it was still moving! He had a seizure and his heart exploded. They crashed into the corner of the motel building that we were in. We heard noises and sirens. We didn't know what the heck it was until she came running in her heels, huffing and puffing like she had seen the devil himself.

She explained to us what happened and that the police were looking for her. We are sitting there in this room and Rico asks, "Babe, did you get his wallet?" she replied, "No. I couldn't get it, but I got all the dope." Oh man. Now we are all looking at each other wondering, "Is this some cursed crack? Is there some rat poison in here?" And then we did the dumbest thing that I have ever seen three people do at once. We all decided to take a hit at the same time from all three pipes in case something happened. Idiots. But nothing happened, except that we got too high. We stayed hidden and sweating in the room for hours while right outside, there was the dead guy in his BMW with the ambulance the police all still trying to figure out what happened!

Once we made it out of there, another crack dealer asked to borrow my car. I told him no and he got mad. The crack dealer began talking to a big African American guy across the street, and before I realized what was going on, the big guy ran across the street and looked at me through the car window, nodded his head and ran back to his hotel room. I asked Rico what that was all about. He said, "Dude. You're marked for death. He's gonna go kill you for that $20 rock, for that dealer." Rico told me to get out of there ASAP! He had done me a huge favor, because I was too high to even notice what was gonna happen!

It was around that time that I was hitting bottom hard. I ended up living in a car on Skid Row in downtown Los Angeles. This is as bad as it gets before you die. Tons of people all out on the street, living in card board boxes and plastic tents, all cracked out and real scary. There had been a tunnel nearby that people were leered into by crackheads, and they were lit on fire. To top it all off, word on the street was that the Cecil Hotel around the corner, notorious for crack and really bad things happening in it, possibly had poisoned water and that people there were getting really sick from drinking it.

We soon found out the real cause of sickness. A young Asian woman was traveling through LA and probably thought she could save some money by staying at the Cecil. Bad idea. She had gotten kidnapped, gang raped and was held captive for a while before she was murdered. The killers decided to drop the body into the water tank of the Cecil Hotel. As the body decomposed, the inhabitants and crackheads got a taste of her, through the faucets. A horrific story and ending. As high as I was, it even shocked the shit out of me and made me sick to my stomach.

Even for us crackheads at the time, the new "meth" craze was scary. We avoided tweakers. How's that for the pot calling the kettle black? But the reason for this is quite simple. Crack comes from cocaine, and once you stop smoking it for a couple of hours, you could start to come down off the high. The scary thing about meth, also known as speed, glass, or "ice," is that you only need a tiny bit and it's so cheap to get, and it keeps you way high for hours and hours. But the fact is, it's made with so many different chemicals, cleaning products and other disgusting substances, that it literally starts to cook and fry your brain. Not that cracks any better, but there's a massive problem in Hawaii now, due to the indigenous people who are addicted to meth. I got a chance to see this while living in Waikiki, as it's called "Ice in Paradise". Not paradise anymore. Meth is a serious global problem.

Demons are real, and even in reference to alcohol, they are known as "spirits". I then realized that I couldn't stop on my own. I looked in the mirror and my skin was turning grey. I was a walking zombie, and slowly dying. I realized that if I didn't stop and get out of there, I could be the next one to end up in someone's glass of water at the Cecil's, or like the firemen, or others who would be dead in the gutter from crack over dose, or stabbed.

Unlike most, I had a car, so people would use me and my car as a dope taxi. They'd pay me in rock, put gas in, and go do their dealings. I had to get out so the next deal I made I tried to make sure that I had enough gas to get far away. They like to crumb you along with little bits of dope to keep you hooked and give only a couple of bucks in gas money so they could keep you around. It's a deadly spider web. On the streets its known as "the game," an art of knowing how to work people for dope. It's satanic.

I knew that I wasn't strong enough to stop. Nothing worked since I was dealing with demons. I had heard that if you mess with them, seven times worse will come upon you. And they sure did. When I was finally able to get out of there, I asked my sister to pay for a hotel in Simi Valley to help me get off the streets of LA. In addition, I had my faithful shepherd named Wolfgang, who had been with me through all of this. And the hotel took pets, thank God.

So, I went in there, cleaned up, and told God, "I can't do this on my own. Please help me." I then talked to Grandma Betty on the phone and said, "Grandma, I need help. Nothing is working. I tried Doctors. I tried quitting. I tried Rehab. I tried everything." My grandma said, "This is seriously demonic; you need to go and get deliverance." Now deliverance is sort of like what some people would say is an exorcism, but it's really not. Exorcisms are attempted in man-made "priest powers", but deliverance can only be done by the King of Kings, and Lord of Lords, Jesus, who has authority over demons.

As my grandma instructed, I went to a place called "The Healing Rooms" and asked for deliverance. They anointed me with oil, which stands for the Holy Spirit and the blood of Jesus. Three little old ladies laid their hands on my shoulders and head, prayed for me, performed spiritual warfare and got those demons off of me and away from me. Now I know what some of you are thinking… Come on! But you know what? I had been battling this for 25 years and when this was done, and they prayed for me, I could feel all of the demons leave instantly. The craving for alcohol and crack and cocaine all left me. And never came back. So, it's real.

About that time, NY, the crack dealer, had given me a call. He said "Drey!" And even though I was white, and he was black, he'd say, "What up my nigga". But not this time. He sounded different and weird. I asked, "Are you sick? You alright?" He said, "I've been in the hospital, man. I had a kind of a stroke." He proceeded to tell me that his wife had left him and taken the kids (finally… he was a crack dealer), but the wife walking out enabled him to be around some crackhead girlfriends.

Once he finished, I said, "Listen to me carefully. Have you ever heard of the Kennedy curse?" He replied that he hadn't. I said, "You have heard of the Kennedy family." He said, "Yes." I explained, "This is how it goes. Joseph Kennedy, the patriarch of the Kennedy family, what some call the "American Royal Family". Ha! Far from it. Joseph Kennedy made his millions by bootlegging alcohol, destroying millions of families and having brothels all over Chicago and America. So, after that, not only was his life cursed, but his sons and his whole family started to get killed and eliminated. That is a fact. That is the Kennedy curse."

You can't expect to do wrong and mess with others and their family and not think that it won't catch up with you someday. No matter how you justify it. I asked him, "What are you gonna do for a living?" He said, "Keep going. Keep selling rock. It's the only thing I know how to do." I asked him about producing music like he said he wanted to, to which he replied, "That won't pay the bills right now." I said, "Man, you're in too deep. God gave you a warning sign and warning shot. Next time it's not gonna be that easy…if there is a next time." He said, "Ok. Yeah."

I got off the phone with him, but remained kind of monitoring his situation. I'd call him to check up, but nobody picked up. That wasn't like him. About a month and a half later, somebody called me on the phone and it sounded like a mentally disabled or autistic person, but in the sound and tone of NY's voice. I could barely understand him on the phone so I got in the car and said, "I'm coming to see you." And all I heard was "Oookkeeee". Upon arriving, I saw what used to be NY.

He was in a wheelchair. One whole side of his face was drooped and frozen. The whole left side of his body was locked up, with his left hand stuck to his side and withered. I couldn't believe what I saw. He got round two and got put out of commission with another stroke. As if that wasn't enough, the crack ho girlfriend and her family had robbed him blind of everything he had, or, everything he bought with blood money. At that point, I heard a still small voice that said, "Take him to West Angeles Church". His gangster wannabe cousin was hanging out with him and I said, "Come on. Help me put him in the car. We are going to a party."

I took them to church. We got there a little late, and you could hear the music playing.

They came along, thinking it was a party, and it was. I began to open the side door near the front of the church and there were African Americans dancing up a storm on stage, worshiping God. All of a sudden, the doors fly open, and all you see is a white boy pushing in an African American in a wheel chair. And I was the only white man in the whole place amongst hundreds of African Americans. But I had been used to that, and this wasn't a bad scene.

They all stopped and looked at me. I just wheeled in NY and we sat in the front row. He couldn't even talk, and could barely move. We sat through the service with hundreds of eyes on us. Apparently, this was too much for the gang "star" cousin, 'cause it was like throwing water on the wicked witch of the west in "The Wizard of Oz." He flew out of there. But that's ok, he was a distraction anyway. At the end of the service they said, "If anyone needs prayer, come up." So, I wheeled NY over, and man, about 5 big African American brothers ran up on me. I thought they were gonna jack me, but they asked, "What's going on?" I told them straight up, "I was a crackhead and have been delivered by God and Jesus. And this is my crack dealer who wouldn't stop. And now God's got him a wakeup call. He needs prayer and he needs it now."

They looked at me, pushed me aside and said, "We got this brother!" and they all jumped in and started praying. At that moment, Kerry, as NY's real name is known, lost it. He couldn't stop crying. Kerry made things right with God, repented of his sins and asked Jesus into his heart as his Lord and Savior. After that, he actually ended up getting better. He saw me go from the streets to an estate, living in Malibu, sober and healthy, and seeing crack head "Drey" turn into "Relentless".

CHAPTER 10

CELEBRITY JUST US

FROM THE TIME I WAS a little kid growing up under the Hollywood sign and around the corner from Jodie Foster her brother, I knew I wanted to work in TV and film. Jodie had already started working on Disney movies and was well known, even as a child. Buddy was working on a show called "Mayberry R.F.D.," a spinoff of the classic, "The Andy Griffith Show".

I would see Buddy riding his Honda 50, racing up and down our private little canyon road and cul-de-sac, and I remember telling my mom, "I wanna be on TV so I can buy a little Honda 50 too." This was a really cool bike at the time and a collector's item now.

Right around the end of my grammar school days, we moved to the San Fernando Valley, which was a good thing. Otherwise, I would have had to attend Le Conte Junior High and then onto Hollywood High, which had turned into Heroin High with LSD, gangs and violence in the 70s. San Fernando Valley was a great place to be; sheltered, but still vast and big enough to run around in. It had lots of opportunity.

Growing up, my parents weren't interested in socializing with Americans. They came from Europe so somehow, they thought they were above Americans. I was born an American and was proud to be one from the time I was a little kid. Anything that said, "Made in America," and had a little American Flag on it was just right for me. And today, I even have the American flag tattooed on my right arm and it says: "Made in America Born Relentless". Everything made in America was the best, still is, and always will be!

We had moved right across the street from a big actor named Stephen Boyd, who is famous for the movie *Ben-Hur*...a classic. There were more entertainment families around me than I could name. One family that I would work with later was Chuck and Charlie Picerni, some of the best stunt drivers in Hollywood.

Around the corner from me lived Cindy Brady, from the "Brady Bunch" TV show, which was huge at the time. Most of those kids would end up being withdrawn because they were so sheltered by private tutors on set. They were used to caterers, limos and having the studio executives kiss their little hineys and pimp them out on TV; when they faced real kids in the real world, they were petrified.

Most of them would end up being ruined for life and their childhood acting career would be put to an end when they realized they weren't wanted anymore once their "cute kid" looks faded. It would shatter their world, and they would end up on drugs and overdosing, just like Dana Plato and Todd Bridges from "Diff'rent Strokes," or Adam Rich from "Eight is Enough," who was breaking into pharmacies. So, I suppose it's good that I didn't become a childhood star, but I almost ended up doing all the other things those childhood stars did. Ouch.

I am now a member of the Screen Actors Guild (SAG). Big deal... they just want to take some of your money. "Union Dues" they call it and want to punish you if you work non-union. They should call it "Screen Communist Guild". I would later make a career out of being a rebel and working non-union. I'd see other people on set that SAG, but were working non-union under fake names; nobody wants to admit it. Well, I raised my hand and I'm proud of it.

That leads me to where I went to next. After finally getting my SAG card, I thought "Oh boy, this is it, the big time. The big money starts now!" Nope. Wrong. Now all you got is a bunch of stuck-up agents, who's only concerns were getting their hands in the pants of cute young girls, any other easy money they could make, and of course, being one of the thousands of next wannabe Brad Pitts!

That's why I'm proud of my non-union heritage. I would go after it, working with stunts, wild animals, guns, weapons, explosions, improv, anything and everything. Non-union people didn't give a shit if you got hurt. It was NON-UNION, meaning no coverage. But it really sharpened my skills so that when I would work near some of the frozen SAG dummies, I would excel.

I perfected the art of the upgrade in many ways. For example, I would set-up on a union set on a bit part, go right to the 1st AD and tell them I was an accomplished and prepared stuntman; I could cover any shots on scenes that the director needed and most importantly, I would stay close by. All the extras and bit part actors are known as an "under 5". That means the production and the director were too cheap to pay you for more than 5 words. They were sitting and trying to impress the girls by reading their fake "scripts". Pretty stupid isn't it? My 5 words would have been: "Stick it up your ass!" But I always had more than 5 words to say.

It had gotten to a point where it was so ridiculous trying to find work. They went from hard copy black and whites being raced around town by carriers to finally going on the internet, which was great because we were able to intercept the Hollywood "sacred scroll,". which were typically the casting call notices that only the elite SAG casting directors were allowed to possess, as if they were some sort of temple priest with the elite scrolls that only they were able to look at. They would do favours for other casting directors, like put their kids and spouses on TV shows. They were like a bunch of scandalous drug dealers, but with casting calls instead of coke.

Here is what I did. I had learned to tithe, giving 10% of my first fruits and money to God's Kingdom, and I was always blessed for that.

The bible says to give, and it shall be given unto you; some people may refer to it as karma. I would get on my knees and pray to God. I said "Lord, be my agent and manager." And from that day on, I never needed an agent or manager. I had an agent but booked jobs on my own. The checks through SAG would automatically go to the agent, who would be in Thailand staying in hotels with young girls for two weeks at a time. I would have to beg for my 85% back and they would have the nerve to tell me, "I'll write you a check in a couple of weeks." As they say in New Zealand: "Get stuffed!" Thanks for nothing V.K.!

It was the most amazing thing to see because I had it all covered across the board, from the casting breakdowns to the casting directors. I went on three or four auditions a day, sometimes three to four days in a row. The other passive chowder head actors just couldn't understand. I was "Relentless". In fact, I got calls from other actors, who had huge agents and couldn't get them in for reads. I would make the calls, get them in, and get them parts. After a while the casting directors started calling me, telling me about a breakdown, inviting me to a casting and even booking me right away for roles without auditions! UNHEARD OF!

One time I booked a job for Fresh Start Rehab Centre in Costa Mesa, where I played a rehab dad who had slipped into alcohol and drugs and was in despair. I went in on the audition improv and nailed it on the first take. They were all amazed at how I "captured the role". Little do they know it was what the NY acting school called "Method Acting." From James Dean, to Marlon Brando and Steve McQueen, "method acting" is capturing the role and actually living it. For example, the way Nicolas Cage captured an Oscar in *Leaving Las Vegas* because he prepared for the role by going to Ireland with his best friend and being drunk and hung over for four to five months. May have worked with alcohol, Nick, but don't try it with heroin or crack!

"Method acting" originated in Russia with Konstantin Stanislavski, prior to the Actor's Studio in New York, and was brought to Hollywood.

Now, it is referred to as "organic acting." You can't use "method acting" for everything, like playing the role of a killer, since you can't really go murder someone, or you shouldn't. It is Howard Fine, again in Hollywood, who has taught it and showed how to perfect it.

Returning to the Rehab dad gig, little did they know that I really was going through the rehab process on and off. When it came time to film a part in a bar, we went to the nice clean offices at Fresh Start in Costa Mesa and then to a seedy bar in Santa Ana, where they said, "This is where you hit bottom and you're leaning on the bar in despair." The director tried to educate me on a few things. I simply told him to be quiet and role camera.

I bought a beer at the bar, loosened my tie and my shirt, started downing the beer and holding my head in my palm while peeling the label off the beer bottle and weeping for all the money I spent on cocaine. The director said: "Cut! Brilliant! I can't believe it. We got what we needed in one take!"

Anyway, moving on, new deal. "Moving on, new deal" in Hollywood means next setup, next shot. I talked to you about Lee Majors on *Fall Guy* when I got my start. Lee was just an amazing guy to work with and he had just broken up with his star wife, Farrah Fawcett Majors, a 70s icon and one of the original Charlie's Angels. He had just come off of binging on cocaine and was known as the "6 Million Dollar Man" from his TV show before that; he probably snorted 6 million dollars' worth of cocaine in his day.

By the way, the Fall Guy Stuntman's Association logo that you see at the top is rare and I got it for working on the show. Some so-called loser friend who was watching my house stole my jacket. It's a blue Fox jacket with white leather sleeves, my initials, A.A., and the Fall Guy patch on the back. I will give a huge reward if anyone finds it. Bigger reward if the person who stole it is turned into a human piñata!

It was very common in the 70s and 80s for everyone to snort way too much cocaine on sets, resulting in an increase in onset deaths as well as really crappy sit-com writing in that era. The writers were all so gacked out on coke that the quality went down in TV shows. I remember my friend was a cocaine dealer at the time, and Sherman Hemsley, from *The Jeffersons,* was in the hospital with heart issues and was sending his assistant to pick up cocaine from my friend. Can you believe that? We just couldn't stop. So, don't start!

David Hasselhoff did too much Peruvian marching powder himself, before he sobered up. Thank God for that, because when he was shooting *Night Rider,* he would be so gacked out that he couldn't talk and would sit in his limo peeking through the window, paranoid until he was ready to come out. As David did more lines, the Night Rider car kit got more lines to speak. We have a saying in Hollywood, "When you are grinding your teeth so hard that enamel dust is flying out of your mouth when you speak, it's pretty much time to stop." David could barely talk at that time, so the car carried the show. Later on, he went off to *Baywatch* and did well and got sober.

When I wasn't working as a stuntman or actor, I tried being an electrician, lighting the sets. We would work on the cat walks, or "the greens" as they were called, above the sets, and face the lights down towards the people. You would fry your forearm when turning the lights and changing them. The famous saying in Hollywood is "hurry up and wait," so you would just sit up there for hours. A guy had partied the night before and was sitting in a chair up there in the greens, asleep with his chair leaned back. They tried calling his name, but he didn't hear it, so they screamed at him. He woke up and tilted his chair forward, not realizing that his leg had gone numb. Do you know that guy fell over and broke his leg up on the greens! At that point I said enough lighting for me. I need to be around the camera.

This all took place at Fox Studios. They filmed a lot of Marilyn Monroe movies there, so you could walk inside the sound stages, see the old dusty super thick walls, feel the history in these amazing sound stages and almost feel the presence of all the famous people that had worked there. It was fascinating to me. Aside from Warner Brothers, 20th Century Fox and Paramount Studios, the mother of all studios was MGM studios, hands down.

Metro-Goldwyn-Mayer, the one with the lion roaring before the intro credit, had the baddest sound stages in the world. They shot all the amazing musicals of the 30s and 40s in these giant sound stages, so they needed to be able to move in massive sets. They even had my favorite sound stage, old number 6. This was known as the world's tallest sound stage and it had to be, because it had the floor that would split in half on rollers and an Olympic sized swimming pool underneath it. It also had to be high because Esther Jane Williams, the high dive movie star, had to be able to dive into the pool from a great height.

MGM was known as the Dream Factory, and it was that. It created some of the greatest movies in the history of Hollywood and all filmmaking. That's why I was so into the older filmmaking process and studios, back when they had talent, skills, morals and movie magic. That's also why my Grandma moved here. You see, in the height of The Great Depression and World Wars, no matter what, 80 million people a week would find a way to get to the movies and escape from the cruelties of their real world.

At its height, MGM boasted more stars than in the heavens, and that included Clark Gable, the Barrymores, Judy Garland, Mickey Rooney, Errol Flynn and Marx Brothers. I could go on forever, but you get it.

I started doing grip work too. My first day was at MGM. From MGM, I went to Lorimar-Telepictures, and then to now Sony Studios, where I would work again many times. The grips maintain all the back drops. We tie off any lines, and are basically riggers of all the sets, and the statement was, "If anyone can, a grip can." Alan Ladd, the famous actor who was really short, used to be a grip; not a good one. He got kicked around by the grips, so, when he became famous and filmed his scenes with Veronica Lake, he ordered all grips off set.

The first day that I worked, somebody had stolen the two granite MGM lions at the main gate. At the time, it was being sold, so nobody payed much attention to the guys with the moving trucks and the clipboard that had stolen a piece of Hollywood history. They have never been recovered and are probably sitting in somebody's private collection. Aaron Spelling, the famous Hollywood producer, offered anybody a lifetime role in his TV shows if they could provide a lead for the recovery of the Lions. Sad ending for MGM, as I saw them hoisting the MGM logo off the top of the world's highest sound stage that same day.

Meanwhile, back at work, the older grips had taken me out for a beer in the middle of the day. I was wondering why they were being so nice; I soon found out. They took me up the longest flight of wooden stairs as there was no elevator, to the top of the inside of the sound stage number 6. It was a grip's job to be able to walk the grids, which were 4x4 foot long beams in the ceiling. They told me that for my initiation, I had to jump over the rail and walk the beams in what is known as "The Ozone." I'm telling you, when you stepped out on that beam, walked across it, and looked down nearly 100 feet to the floor below, you felt like you were in the ozone. Once at the end, you were to carve your initials into the beam as a rite of passage. My nickname at that time was "Hollywood Up High". Yet again, I said to myself, if I'm gonna take risks like this, I'd rather do it in front of the camera on high falls!

Over the next couple of days, I took an understanding to what the word "go hide" meant. I had been working and wanted to make my mark, so I hustled. It was always in me to work hard. It was the middle of the night and raining. I was riding a cruiser bike from one sound stage to another, loving life and singing in the rain. I thought that was the big time for me until I got to my destination and the key grips told me, "Come here. You don't need to work so hard." They said "It's your turn. Go hide." When I asked them what that meant, they replied, "We will cover for you. Go get lost for a while." So, they had this hidden room in the corner of the soundstage where they were snorting, smoking pot and drinking beers out of an ice chest in the middle of a frickin' rainy night at MGM studios, all the while, making bank. Welcome to Hollywood!

In order to become what was referred to as "a permit," you had to work 30 days, but not in a row. When you worked your 30 days, you could be eligible to be a full-time grip. Doesn't sound like much, but it's almost near impossible unless you have a friend or an uncle director getting you days on sets. And I had neither. I would see knuckle-head director's nephews show up with a hammer and a rope tied around their waist to hold it up. On the other hand, I would have a full tool bag and leather gloves. At the end of the day, these other guys would have either smashed their hand or cut it with an electric saw, which I have seen happen. Can you guess who would get the 30 days? Still not me. So, I said, "Screw all of this. I'm not trying to do this for a pension plan like everyone else." It was time for me to move on and get back in front of the camera. All this grip stuff and "go hide" wasn't working for me. I was in it to win big time!

I had made a habit of going to all the major studios and sound stages. I would visit every sound stage from ex-Burbank, and especially Warner Brothers, to see the sound stage where *Casablanca* was filmed since Bogart was such a big influence on me.

There were almost a hundred movies put out by Warner Brothers that year, yet *Casablanca* stood out. No special effects, no green screen, nothing complicated. Just the straight-forward, awesome black and white movie made by Julius and his brother. I learned how to write and edit as they did. I found out they would write the scenes, put the pieces of paper down on the ground, look at them, pick them back up and number them. That's how they came up with their formula for editing and filming *Casablanca* (my favorite movie). Brilliant, yet it was simple and it worked. And it still does.

Later, I would get to re-create the famous scene of Rick saying goodbye to Ilsa at the rainy, misty, foggy airport.

There was a group of us hustlers in Hollywood, who, before the internet was used for casting, would call each other on the telephone to tell each other about the call for the casting agencies and what they had booked for the next day. For example, the TV show "Weird Science" had a call for four vampires for the next morning. My friend Chaz had booked a bit part as a vampire. We would crash the sets like a party and tell the first AD, who was so confused in the morning anyway, that casting had sent us over. It almost always worked because they didn't have time to call casting, and it was always for certain that somebody would be late or not show up.

The AD would just give in and give us a SAG voucher, and we would cross off the name on top and put our own. I became a lead vampire on that show and worked with a girl who was, at the time, Miss Texas or something. Now she's Krista Allen. She went a long way and almost ended up marrying George Clooney. But this was a regular thing for us. It was all about beating the system to get on set, and the art of the upgrade. Could we milk them for a stunt? A smoke bump (getting extra money from them for working around smoke)? Could we hit them for SAG OT, or gold time (over time and a half)? Could we get the ultimate upgrade, a regular role or a key scene with key lines? We were all just having such a great time!

It was interesting for me because I was probably one of the only 1% born and raised in Hollywood, California. Everyone else was either a big fish in their small pond town of Hicksville, with someone telling them, "Boy, you should go to Hollywood," or some chick who won a local contest and somebody told her "You'll be a star!"

Hollywood is an absolute meat grinder. It will pull you in, grind you into hamburger and leave you rotting on the side of the road in the gutter. Since the start of Hollywood, there have been so many shattered dreams of men and women who have ended up dead by overdose, suicide or wounded up in porn. And that's the real truth. Only 1-2% of Hollywood actors make enough to live on or even get insurance from SAG. You have to make over $6,000 a year to even qualify for SAG insurance. But soon, none of you will have to worry about that in Hollywood since China's gonna run the entertainment business and lead the way. They don't put up with trash TV or promote it to their people. The world is changing in a big way, and not for the better. So, let's make the most of it now.

I had gotten a phone call from a personal trainer friend of mine. He said he knew a guy named Ray Anthony Williams, who had written the movie *The Fast and the Furious*. I met with him and he told me his story. Ray was an African American guy who worked as a courier and messenger for Universal Pictures. Ray had written a script titled *BET*. It was the true story of his father and him racing real V8 muscle cars in the city of Inglewood and in the Deep South. He had handed the script to a man named Brett Carroll at Universal, and in return, had a piece of paper from Brett Carroll with his phone numbers and even his home number after he received the script.

After constant and repeated phone calls to Brett and his associates, Ray was completely ignored and let go at Universal. He was sitting in his car, stuck in traffic on the freeway, when he heard a man on the radio named Vin Diesel, someone who had made his career and fortune off of the stolen property of Ray Anthony Williams! He even recited the famous "10 seconds or less" line from Ray's script! 10 seconds or less stands for a length of a quarter mile that you would cover in a drag race.

Ray was sick to his stomach, however, he went and saw the movie. Sure enough, they had stolen the whole script. I was in shock and couldn't believe it. I had so many pieces that I'd wrote stolen from me before, but this was just blatant robbery. I told him that I would help him and see what I could do. He said every time he called the VP or anyone's office, they completely ignored him and never called him back.

I told him at quarter to 2 PM that I would make that phone call myself. I prayed, called the head offices at Universal and was able to connect with the VP at that time. He had just come back to his office to grab something and his assistant wasn't there, so he said he picked up the phone.

When he asked what the call was in regard to, I explained the situation and how serious it was. He agreed to see us in the board room at Universal the following week. That movie that you see about a candy ass group of wanna-be Feds in imported cars is all bullshit. If you ever went down to the real hood, Paul Walker and Vin Diesel types would get their asses bitch slapped and their cars pulled from them... and that's just from the girls! It was such a joke watching this movie. Universal had justified stealing Ray's script because the Writer's Guild of America states that you can take and change 60% of somebody else's work and call it your own! This was, and still is, insanity to me. How would you like it if I stole your whole car but re-painted it, changed the interior, the rims and tires, and now, it belongs to me? It's the exact same thing.

They justified it by making it with rice burners, Japanese cars, instead. The real American Muscle Car V8 has been, and always will be, King of the Quarter Mile. The NDRA (National Drag Racing Association), Hot Rod Association and any real drag racer were livid and furious to hear the claim in the movie that these little Japanese cars were the "King of the Road".

I grew up with Muscle cars. Ray's original script is 100 times better than any of the *Fast and Furious 7* or whatever they are on now. They are getting so ridiculous. Just making the movie the way Ray meant it to be would be simple and more raw, but I can't say anymore lest the ideas get stolen again!

Ray and I called Lonnie, the owner of Inglewood Speed Shop, and the real boys from the hood. We asked them to show up at the Universal meeting and bring their man cars, not boy cars. They brought all

American V8 muscle with superchargers, blowers and uncorked headers (racing mufflers). Some of these cars were so badass that they weren't even street legal, which was Ray's point to the whole movie. Ray's dad had a '69 Chevelle Malibu with a 4 speed and would stick a $100 bill on the dash board. As a little boy, he told Ray, "You can keep that hundred dollar bill son, if you can grab it off the dash board before I shift all 4 gears." In those days, where Ray grew up in the south, four telephone poles equalled a quarter mile!

Ray never got that hundred dollar bill, but he ended up in the back seat a couple of times. You have no idea the torque and the power of the V8 muscle car; neither did Universal. We explained the situation, and they played the card I thought they were gonna play: If you change 60 % of something, blah blah blah. So, I asked the executives to step over to the windows. I said, "You have done America a great injustice by lying to the public, stimulating the Japanese car market, and spitting in the face of real men, Feds, and drag racers." We pointed downstairs and I asked the boys over my cell phone to fire up the V8s. When they did, the glass rattled on the top floor of that executive building in Universal!

The executives had a pale look on their faces as they came downstairs scared as shit, but met the boys from the hood. What happened was unbelievable. You would think that they would give Ray something, but if they admitted anything they would have to admit to all of it.

We tried to call all kinds of attorneys to go after Universal, but came to find out the other dirty little side of Hollywood…stealing is 50% of the industry. You take an intellectual property, sign your name to it and it's a legal license to steal. For the last 80 years, they have put a hundred dollar retainer in every law firm in Los Angeles.

So, when I went to sue Universal, the attorneys that were any good told me, "There's a conflict of interest. We have a retainer from Universal. They are our clients". Worse than a bunch of frikkin Chicago mobsters. To add insult to injury, they realized what we had said was true about the muscle cars and the candy assess they had as actors. In response, they bumped it up after they talked to us and added Dwayne Johnson and real muscle cars as their attempt to man up the next couple of movies of the *Fast and Furious* property.

I got us on a TV show called *Celebrity Justice*, hoping that the situation would be straightened out. When we went on the show, they were using the "race card" on Ray, calling him an "angry black man"; well guess what, I was an "angry white man". They filmed Ray and me at the muscle car shop, Inglewood Speed Shop. I asked Ray to bring me a copy of the script and put a pink cover on it. He thought I was crazy. I said, "I'll explain on camera". As we were sitting there with the muscle car behind us and the hood open, I started to talk about the theft and the 60% nonsense mentioned above. When I got to the analogy of stealing somebody's car, I said "At the end of the day, Ray Anthony Williams still owns the pink slip (ownership papers) to this vehicle, known as *BET*, aka the *Fast and the Furious*." We are not done with Hollywood yet. When I talked to my friend and mentor, James Cameron, about the script, he said, "Don't worry or trip out. Muscle car movies will never go out of style. Take your time and film it right." And we will!

 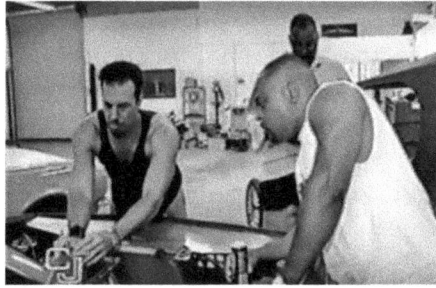

It's sad about Paul Walker and his death in the flaming red Ferrari that he was burnt alive in, but he wouldn't be dead had he not been in a stolen vehicle movie. The curse had begun and will continue until "celebrity justice" is served! Ray had to work two to three jobs to support his three kids, all the while, people are driving around at Universal and other production companies in stolen cars, with stolen money in bank accounts. A whole industry made BILLIONS of dollars because of an unknown Ray Anthony Williams. Ray is a God-fearing man and God's vengeance will be exacted on the people who stole from him. I promised him that one day we will make the movie the way it was supposed to be made and spank Universal's butts at the box office. We'll show them how real American Muscle Cars and gangsters perform, react and live. What Universal and Hollywood currently promote is all a façade. Even Vin Diesel, who seems so tough on camera with his bald head and raspy voice, quit doing MMA with Grand Master Sensei Gokor Chivichyan because he couldn't handle the real thing!

One night I was working as a Colorado State Trooper on *All About Steve* with Sandra Bullock in one of her first directing debuts. Sandra, much respect to you. Sandra had gone on over 440 or so auditions without ever landing a role. Finally, being persistent or "Relentless", she's done very well for herself.

It was 4AM when the casting director called me. They loved me because I would give them the inside skinny on what was happening, what we were filming on set and how stupid everyone else was getting. People turned working on set into their own big parties. When the casting director called me, I mentioned, for future reference since it was the last day on set, that I worked with weapons, that I'm Russian, etc. I thought nothing of it and hung up the phone. Within 5 minutes, the phone rings and she's on the other line saying, "Wait a minute. You said you shoot real guns for the military?" I told her I yes. She asked, "You are Russian?" to which I again replied yes. She asked, "You're a stuntman?" I said yes. She asked, "Have you ever done double shifts? And I replied, "Haven't you read my book on the topic?" She laughed and finally said, "Very good. Can you be at Sony Studios on set at 6AM?" "Ma'am, I gotta super charged Jaguar. I'll make that call."

Before I we hung up with one another, she urged, "Listen to me carefully. Do not bring a cell phone or a camera on set. Do not tell anybody what you are working on, and I mean anybody. Guys are dropping like flies and are being fired on that set as we speak. People that know better are even getting caught up in this." "What's the big deal?" I asked. She says to me, "Steven Spielberg and George Lucas have been going out of their way to conceal the fact that they are filming *Indiana Jones, the Kingdom of the Crystal Skull.* There is a myth and rumour going around in the media that they are about to film it, or are going to try to film it. They are 2 months in. Can I trust you and count on you?" With a Russian accent, I said, "Da. Is good." She laughed, and I was on my way to the old MGM lot, now known as the Sony studios.

I was excited, and it clearly showed as I showed up to the set early. I had been wanting to work with Spielberg and Lucas and had even prayed to my manager agent, God, about it in detail. And it happened. As I got there, I was fitted for a 50s period peace, Russian military soldier.

At that point, all of the other extras started to show up and were being fitted for their Russian military outfits. The stunt coordinator walked in and said, "Do any of you have any real military weapons experience, particularly in the AK47?" Everyone was dumbfounded. He said, "I will know if you lie". I raised my hand confidently. He asked, "You. Where?" I answered back, "Two Nine Palms, Sir! United States Marine Corps aggressor role player, AK47 Specialist." He said to me, "I'm a United States Marine Corps Sergeant. Two nine is my home base. You sir, come with me right away." I got a bunch of dirty looks from the girls dressed in the Russian military outfits as I got upgraded to stuntman AK47 weapons expert, and got put in key shots with Harrison Ford. While everyone else was holding fake rubber AK47s, the armourer gave me a real one to carry around and shoot with blanks. Now, I felt comfortable and at home.

It was at that point that I walked into their giant sound stage and seen how they had made the whole South American Amazon jungle come alive.

I'm talking about real trees, plants, animals, sand and Russian Military Camps. It was unbelievable! However, the energy was just was thrown off as everyone was trying to jockey in position in front of the camera. All of these Russian soldiers pushing and shoving…it just looked stupid. I stuck to myself, walking around and just breathed, meditated, relaxed, and prayed, waiting until the scene cleared and the directors called out, "Moving on. New deal." All of the previous extras left the stage with attitudes.

A man with an English accent walked in, looked at me said, "You really look the part." "I'm really Russian," I told him. He said "I can tell. You're holding the rifle properly." He proceeded to ask, "Is that one of the real ones?" "Yes Sir." He instructed, "Good. Come with me. Stand on this mark and wait." As the other people poured back into the sound stage for the new take, again, everyone was bunched up and trying to get in front of the camera, which was really annoying. At that moment, the guy with the English accent came in and yelled at everyone, "Clear the set!" and like a pack of jackals, they all scampered off; except for me, I stood on my mark. He nodded his head, "Good."

I had turned to my left for a moment and looked around the sound stage. I could see, hidden in the jungle, video village. Video village is all the multiple monitors and control centre for the director and producer. One thing you should never do is look over the director or producer's shoulder while they are either filming or looking at the scenes. My friend but chowder-head, Anthony De Longis, known as "the master of the whips," made a tragic career error on this same movie.

Anthony had been hired to work with Indie, Harrison Ford on his bullwhip skills. During the time Harrison Ford was trying to nap, Anthony was putting on a bullwhip cracking show for all of the extras. He is a former theatre actor who loves to be in character. Harrison Ford was not amused; nor was Steven Spielberg. Anthony had a chance of a lifetime to work regularly with *DreamWorks* and *Lucas Films*. This was his dream job. He is the world's best bullwhip guy and even has his own instructional video, but sometimes, you gotta know when to sit down and shut up. Consider that strike one.

The second strike he never got. It went from strike one to strike three... and YOUR OUT! Strike three was one of the stupidest moves that I think I'd seen anyone in Hollywood make. Anthony had decided that he wanted to sharpen his giant bowie knife right behind Steven Spielberg while he was at video village. Needless to say, it freaked him out. That was about the time that they caught the guy who was stalking Steven Spielberg. He has been making death threats to Steven Spielberg and even said that he wanted to sodomize him. Detectives found a ski mask, duct tape and knives in the guy's car. Spielberg said to his assistant, the first AD with the English accent, "Who is that guy?!" He told him, "He's your whip expert." Spielberg said, "No he's not. Lose him." That was it. Game over.

I turned back around from Video Village and almost bumped a guy in the head. He was wearing a fedora and a brown leather jacket. Sticking out his hand to me, he said, "Excuse me. Harrison." "Andre. Nice to meet you Sir." He said, "Please don't call me Sir." It was in that moment that I realized I was in a key shot. Not only that, but Karen Allen, who was in the original Indiana Jones, was brought back to play Shia's mom. I was speaking to her outside and she was very nice, so when she walked into the sound stage, she looked at me and said, "Hi Andre!" like I was part of the family. I felt comfortable around Karen and Harrison.

Next, a lady walks in playing a Russian officer. It was Cate Blanchett, carrying a sword. All of this was just so overwhelming; I wanted a picture of this. I was tempted to sneak a camera in but didn't. That still small voice told me not to. But later, on Monday morning, what I didn't realize was that the onset photographer for *Lucas Film* and *DreamWorks* had taken a picture of us, and it was released into the LA times. They weren't hiding the story anymore and it was the first photo they released. I as beyond blessed to be in it.

That was one of the best sets that I had ever worked on. When the camera rolled, Cate, who was highly caffeinated, turned around with that sword so close, I thought she was going to poke my eye out. She gave orders in Russian to retrieve Karen Allan at gunpoint. A lot of fun. I would go on to do stunts in the movie and many other additional scenes.

My favorite part was that all day, Spielberg would come out from behind video village, smoking a Cuban cigar, and talk to me and Harrison. Harrison would have a Cuban cigar burning too, setting it down in between takes. I loved a good Cuban cigar, so the next day, I came back with my Cuban cigars, along with my newest invention of the *cigar event*, a little chrome devise that would hold your cigar upright like a big pen holder so you wouldn't need to set it down and have it roll off. Each came in little velvet bags, and I gave a custom one to both Harrison and Steven.

Everyone but the main cast, Spielberg, and George Lucas hated me, including the other Russian soldiers included. That's how I knew I was in the right place, doing the right thing. Hollywood is full of haters. It was a Friday evening and my friends called me saying, "Dude! You gotta go out with us tonight. Come on! You've been workin' too much. There's a super cool party and event." I said, "If you can beat what I'm doing right now, I'll leave." When they asked me what I was doing, I told them, "I'm dressed as a Russian soldier, holding a real AK, about to do a stunt. I'm smoking a Cuban cigar with Harrison Ford and Steven Spielberg. I'm eating a giant golf-ball sized, honey covered coconut macadamia nut and the Starbucks truck just pulled up on set to deliver for all of us. I had a snow crab omelette for breakfast, lobster and filet mignon for lunch and I think George Lucas is talking about some Greek falafels being delivered any minute. So, if you don't mind, I'm gonna get back to the real party." I heard on the other line, "Shut up. I hate you. Ok then, you can stay."

I found myself on a Saturday afternoon feeling really good about my decision not to go out that night to party. This was what I was born to do, so nothing else could have replaced it. As I was walking down Zuma Beach at Sunset, sober and happy, I was smoking a Cuban cigar and decided to talk to my agent again. I said, "God, while we are on a roll here, I'd really like to work with Clint Eastwood and Ron Howard" (I was big on speaking things into existence, and still am). And that's exactly in the order that my prayers were answered.

Monday, my phone rang again with the casting agents on the other line. They said they had a period piece film for me to work on. I love period piece movies, and they always worked well for me. I consider myself a real man, not a metrosexual Hollywood type, so I don't have to look super lean or have to have the coolest haircut. Nothing worse than seeing a cop or S.W.A.T. or a Russian soldier played by a model looking guy. It just doesn't work. Imagine Tobey Maguire playing "Spider-Man"; I'm sorry, but they should have just called it "Spider-Boy." Hollywood likes to replace manly roles with boys, and it's just not realistic. God made you an original, why do you want to be a cheap copy of someone else? I had learned early on that nobody could be you or better than you. I locked onto that notion like a pit bull.

I had been called to Burbank, one of the largest wardrobe departments, and as I got there, it was about quarter to 5PM and here we go with the same model-type, prima-donna guys. They were all standing in a huge group, complaining about how they needed to go first because they had another modelling audition to attend. They were acting worse than bitches, and I do mean female dogs (I don't want to offend women).

By the time I walked in, the wardrobe guy and his assistants were swamped with whiny-hineys and in a rush to outfit everyone for the movie. When I walked up, he held up his palm. He said, "You need to wait!" I clearly saw that the man was stressed, and I understood the nature of the animals he was working with, so I replied, "Sir, I am in no rush. I will go sit down. Call me whenever you are ready." Everyone else looked at me and kind of whispered "Good" underneath their breath. I said, "Ladies First!"

The man had finished working with the huge group of guys and I could tell he was mad. He just pretty much started throwing clothes at them. Those guys were dumb because they got all the drab, gangly, knotted up shoes and grey wool pants of the 1920s that this guy had. But when he came to me, and I was still patient and waiting, he said, "You… I have something special for. You have a natural build and you are a larger sized man (not needing to look skinny and model looking paid off). I have a special custom Royal blue suit with a white round arrow collar, used only once by Ving Rhames. It will fit you perfectly."

I put that thing on…it was made for me and I looked like a million bucks. My patience had paid off. I remember my friend wanting me to go out and drink with him that night. He was jealous that I was going to work on *The Changeling* with Clint Eastwood, Angelina Joli, and John Malkovich, so he kept me drinking all night and told me to call in sick. I felt so bad in the morning that for one of the first times, I called the casting director and said that I was sick and wasn't going to show. They had seen the picture of me in the blue suit, and I was cast as one of the few LA City councilmen, as I was told on the phone that morning. So, I had a coffee, got my act together, and went in. I had almost missed an opportunity of a lifetime.

I felt much better once I got on set. As I got there and put on my suit, they placed us in our positions in the courtroom scene. Clint Eastwood looked at us (the LA Councilmen) and the first AD walked over to me and said, "Clint says you really sell this shot. Come with me." I was placed in one of the desks, which was one of the best spots. Later, I'd be able to talk with Clint and tell him that he was my childhood motivation for shooting guns, and a role model for me. He thanked me and the ice was broken. He had a giant parrot, a cockatoo, that he would have on his arm, on set. I told him I was an animal handler trainer as well.

So, when he would go and set it down, guess who he started leaving it with? Yeah, me. It was then that I had walked over and heard about Steve. Steve is the Camera Operator and Director of Photography (D.P.) and Clint goes to him, unashamedly, for every shot and whispers to him. A smart director is never afraid to admit that he asks the D.P.'s opinion on every shot. Spielberg wasn't, Clint wasn't and neither was Ron Howard. James Cameron also taught me to be that way, walking and talking every shot over with my D.P.

Clint was the most amazing Director that I had ever seen. He doesn't yell "Action!" or "Cut!" out loud, nor does he have annoying ADs who are trying to prove something by yelling it out themselves. Rather, Clint has his own way of doing things. One scene, he looked at us, and very smoothly said "Now I'd like to get a really good rehearsal. Do your best."

We did the full rehearsal. And then we hear, "New deal. Moving on." And we all said, "Wait! We just rehearsed that scene so good! You're not gonna film it?" and Steve would say, "We just did." That's how Clint does it. You're relaxed, and without the pressures of being in your own head and listening to your subconscious. You've become interested in what you are doing and therefore, you become interesting and natural to watch. I didn't realize it at the time, but I was going to the finest Film School in the world, with the best instructors and experiences on the planet, bar none!

In case you have never seen "The Changeling", it's a horrific story of the real kidnappings and murders of children by Northcott. Angelina Jolie plays the mom, who has been placed inside an insane asylum by the L.A.P.D. to silence her because they had done nothing about the case, due to the initially kidnapped victims all being the children of migrant workers. When a white child got kidnapped, all hell broke loose and the L.A.P.D. had to answer for it. Based on a true story.

I was at the crafts service table and Angelina Jolie was standing there alone. She was petite, but intimidating to some. I asked, "Has anyone talked to her yet?" They said, "No. You don't do that." "Oh really?" Well, I did with Snoop Dog, and I was on my way again.

I walked over to her while everyone was backed up, staring at me. She's just another human being, and we are equal in God's eyes. I'm not intimidated. I said hello and introduced myself. Then I said, "You know, at first when you started acting, since you were Jon Voight's daughter, people didn't take you seriously, and even took you as a joke." She was quiet, and just stared at me. "But you have now become the actor's actor. An example of the industry standard, how acting should be done." Then, she started smiling. She said, "Thank you very much." I then said, "But I'd really like to pray for what is most important, and that is your mission and calling around the world for your children and the other children you work with." She reached out and grabbed my hands, and her eyes started to tear up. She said, "Thank you so much. That's the nicest thing I'd heard in a long time."

I worked late on that shot as Steve, the camera operator, wanted to do additional pick up shots and asked me to stay on set. I did, but had missed lunch. It was worth it. They had called in a caterer, a Greek guy named Toni from Toni's catering. Toni is the celebrity caterer and the biggest in the business use him. Toni had just come off the set of *Indian Jones and the Crystal Skull.* He was always quiet, but polite. But this time, when he saw me coming, he said to everyone "Here comes Andre, the next biggest producer, director and actor in Hollywood." I couldn't help but think, "Wow." He said to me, "You missed lunch, didn't you?" I said, "Yes, Toni. Do you have a piece of bread or a sandwich for me?" He told me no and put his palm on his chest. "I personally will go make my shrimp scampi for you my friend." So, here I am at the end of a great shoot, working with Angelina, John, Steve, Clint and his Parrot. It was that day that I realized I had started to become somebody in the industry.

After I had finished working with Steve, and as everyone else was leaving, I heard "Martini Shot!" Martini shot means last shot of the day. After that, martini time! Everyone loves to hear the phrase martini shot, and everyone shuts up to make sure they get the shot with no noise.

This was around the time that I got a call to be a stunt double for John Travolta. Now John, you're cool and all, but you are a really weird dude. I had been watching John Travolta's career since he was younger. It took a pause right before it died, then somebody named Quentin Tarantino used a defibrillator to revive it. *Pulp Fiction* had brought John back; but something wasn't the same. John would make sure that nobody ever referred to him as John., but refer to him as J.T. But even J.T., if you said it on set, could get you fired. On the call sheet, it would say "Charlie." A call sheet is the list of all the actors, producers, directors, on set talent, stunts, caterer, everyone's call time. You would never find John Travolta's, or J.T.'s name on a call sheet, so Charlie was his call sign.

I get on set, and I'm ready to go as a stunt double for him. I got all my gear and I'm pleasantly surprised because I'm working with one of my favorite people that I had ever met in Hollywood. Robin Williams is someone I respect and love and had been watching as a kid. By the way, Robin RIP. I hope you're with God so I can see you again. I lost another one to suicide, if that's what really happened. It's such a shame for a man to live every minute of his life knocking himself out to make other people happy, and then to go out like this. It made a lot of people sad.

Robin Williams had been the king of improv and I just love that because I live life unscripted, much like he did. Robin's idol and mentor was the famous comedian, Jonathan Winters, who was the emperor of improv. These 2 were so good that nobody could ever keep up with them. There was never a dull moment, and you would borderline think you're going crazy just listening to them.

It was Jonathan Winters who actually got released from an insane asylum to finish his career wonderfully. Was he really insane? Or was everyone else just on a flat-line level? Nobody will really know, but Robin picked up where Jonathan left off. Due to my ADD and dyslexia, I was very comfortable around Robin and his turbo humour; I love being with another improv creative guy that didn't go off of anybody's script.

As I got on set, something really strange happened. The directors, producers and the script supervisor approached me and said, "Here's the script. We need you to read all of Charlie's (J.T.'s) lines and do all of the scenes with Robin, and when Charlie shows up, we need you to walk him through all of the scenes and explain to him where you hit every beat (means beginning and ending your lines) and at what marks (the marks are the places on the floor where you stop, deliver your lines, and keep moving)."

They said, "We are going to film all of it, show it to Charlie when he gets here at video village and you can help him along." I looked at everyone and I thought it was Robin's joke on me. I asks, "Are you guys serious?" They said, "Very serious. We will give you a couple minutes to highlight the script if you need to." I had never heard of this, so I asked them, "How much am I getting paid?" They told me the same amount. I said "Oh great. Thanks a lot." Robin really made me feel comfortable and said, "Let's just have fun with it." The script supervisor said, "I know this is very unusual and uncomfortable, but please do your best." Hey SAG, where were you guys on this one? You see what I mean?

I wanted to be able to look at Robin Williams, act and maintain a dialogue without having to stare down at the script with my glasses on, as if it's a cold read. It was a good opportunity. I had learned from a casting director once, "I would rather you throw down the script, take off your reading glasses, and give me the character. We will work on dialogue later". That's exactly what I did.

I glanced at the page and memorized what I could; improv with Robin on the rest. We rolled and had a fun time. It was a long scene, shot to look like Central Park, and once the crane and the dolly cam stopped moving, I heard a couple people clapping. I looked up, and at the top of the crane cam, I hear a loud voice, "Hey Andre! Great Job! By the way, you looked amazing in the Changeling!" It was Steve, Clint Eastwood's camera man. Very reassuring.

We kept working and filming, but Robin was just too much. He had one scene where a soccer ball rolls over to him. 10 feet away, there's a little boy standing there going, "Hey Mr.! A little help?" Robin runs over and kicks the soccer ball hard, and it plasters the kid in the side of the face. I swear, the kid almost did a backflip, and not a curled up one, I'm talking about a flat one. Robin didn't mean to do it, but he kept going with the flow and yelled out like it was part of the scene, "Sorry mom!" with this hand up, and got behind me. It was so natural for him.

Somebody yelled out during the scene break after he kicked the soccer ball, "Hey Robin, don't you know you could get sued for harassment?" Right away, out of nowhere, Robin goes into this Russian accent and he said "Harassment? No Harassment! Iz like living in Russia with the KGB. I'm on bus, I see this woman. I get off bus. KGB arrest me. They say you harass a woman on bus. I say no! I touch her breast, I touch her legs, I touch everything. But I no touch her ass. So, no her-ass-ment!"

By now, Robin and I are now trading jokes like 2 boxers sparring, and the hours are flying by. About that time, Charlie (J.T.) shows up. His head is bald (he has a couple little stubbles sticking up), and he is hours late. By the time he gets out of makeup, they glue a brown rug onto his head, did a bunch of patchwork, and he didn't have time to be on time, but he did have time to shake the hands of the younger male extras, if you know what I mean. That's his business, but when you shake somebody's hand, you need to let go after about 30 seconds, ok? Spooky. Good thing the KGB wasn't around.

I proceed to tell J.T. where to go, where to stand, what to say and how to say it…and then show him the film. Hollyweird truly. I have no problem working with J. T and I think it's great that he's an accomplished 747 pilot, but he had the same glazed eye look that Tom Cruise has, and I think it's because of that whole weird scientology cult thing. Seriously dudes, there's not going to be any alien mothership picking you up soon, and any religion based on a 30s science-fiction writers needs to be reviewed and disintegrated with a ray gun.

Sure enough, just as I had prayed and in the order I had asked, I got to work with Steven Spielberg, Clint Eastwood, and now, Ron Howard. How did that happen? Well, Tom Hank's regular stunt double was working on another project, so I got called in and interviewed. I had received the news a couple of weeks later, and came to find out that the director of the film is none other than my childhood legend in TV and Film, Ron Howard. I had grown up watching Ron Howard on *The Andy Griffith Show*, Disney Movies, and one of my favorite TV shows, *Happy Days*, that includes not only Ron Howard as Richie Cunningham, but also Fonzie, or the Fonz. Tom liked to do as much of his own stunts and doubling that he could, and Ron would ask him, "Is this something you are comfortable with or could do?" Sometimes Ron would say, "I would really like Tom to do this. How could we do it?" It was awesome. We would make it happen one way or another and I didn't mind stepping in at all.

Working with Tom Hanks was a pleasure. He was not only a gentleman, but was also great to talk to; we would sit there for hours while Ron went over the scenes with Tom. Watching these great directors work and how they think…again, I have to say, was the best film school in the world. I don't know if Ron was a genius producer, or that he had been doing this his whole life, but it was inevitable that he would become great.

Get Smart was one of my favorite TV shows in the 60s, played by Don Adams. He was the original TV version of *Inspector Gadget*, complete with a really cool shoe phone, the original cone of silence and his secret agent assistant who would always malfunction. Everything on his show would malfunction; that's what made it so funny. In addition, he was pitted up against an organization known as "Chaos". These were TV shows where the US would fight *against* organizations around the world like "Chaos", as opposed to today, where our government actually causes and creates it.

Steve Carell from the movie *The 40 Year Old Virgin* was rising high in the comedy ranks. When the remake of the original TV show was going to be done into a movie by the famous director, Peter Segal, and Warner Brothers, I thought, as so many Hollywood remakes are so poorly done, that they don't do the TV show justice. When I heard that Steve Carell was going do it, I felt confident that it was going to be good.

At that time, I was rescuing German Shepherds from Shephard Rescue and training K9 units. When the casting call came out for not only a K9 bomb Squad Cop, but somebody that owned a shepherd, I was more than happy to pimp my dog out to work together. I was excited to work with them and get on set, as my scene was to scout the location around the Disney concert hall on 1st and Grand. The evil organization Chaos had planted a bomb somewhere and it was up to me and the bomb sniffing dog to find it. I had wanted to use the shepherds from the Shepherd Rescue, only caring that the Shepherd Rescue would be on the credits of the film. The stories that would come out of the shepherd rescue were heart breaking at best.

Goldie was the last dog that I had picked up from Shep Rescue. Some maniac in Inglewood, probably on crack, had taken a knife and cut off all four of her pads on the bottom of her feet. It took me about a year of changing bloody socks twice a day to get the bottom of her feet stable. I wanted to use Goldie on that set, so I did.

I was suited up as a cop and on set with cameras rolling. After the scene, the dog's job was to sniff everyone's purses and bags as they entered the concert hall. At the end of the shot, a grip had walked by me and tapped my dog on the back of her head without either one of us facing him. As soon as he did that, coming up from behind like he did, the dog naturally spun around, growled and snapped to defend me, as she should.

The only thing that 100 people had seen and heard, including the director, Peter, and producers, was the last second of Goldie growling and snapping at a crew member. It was a setup. It was a little later that the assistant director and producers approached me and asked, "Can you bring another German Shepherd tomorrow that's not so violent?" The fur raised on my back and I got on my hinds for the rest of the movie.

I would spend Saturday afternoons going to Shep Rescue, donating my time to train these shepherds to be able to go to family homes. Most of them were there, not because of themselves, but by stupid, self-centred, incompetent owners that shouldn't own a plastic parakeet, let alone any kind of dog. These dogs thrown into a back yard, raised without love or attention, then thrown into the shelters for being "uneducated or unruly". Yeah, real fair.

So, I was very upset, and I voiced my opinion to the producers, directors and especially the grip who later told me it was all his fault and that he knew better. I asked him, "Do you realize how serious this is now?" That afternoon and evening, he explained the whole situation to Peter Segal, Warner Brothers and the producers, all of whom were heartbroken at Goldie's story. When I showed up on set the next day, the director and producer called a meeting for the whole set (around 80 people) and announced, "We at Warner Brothers and the producers and directors of *Get Smart* apologize to Andre, Goldie, and German Shepherd Rescue, and are giving Andre and Shep Rescue our onset photographer to take any kind of publicity pictures he wants to help him and promote

Shephard Rescue." I guess they had thought about it. Hollywood was concerned about a lash back from animal lovers, and as well they should be.

An officer with a badge came on set and asked for all the permits for all of the shepherds; we had more than 3. Some Hollywood animal training outfit had showed up with their shepherds. The officer was in the midst of shutting down the set, which he could do since the permit in downtown LA was not proper for all of these German shepherds to work. Fortunately for them, I saved their bacon in return on the movie because the officer recognized me from a couple of weeks ago. I was also training horses at that time and we were doing a shoot for the band "Nickelback," where they wanted 5 horses running down the middle of the street on Broadway in Downtown LA.

We did it at night and I remember it being a wild shoot because the police wanted to shut it down, concerned that the horses wouldn't all stop where they were supposed to; they thought they would keep going and run into traffic. I assured the police that as head wrangler (wearing my cowboy hat that night), all the horses would follow one lead horse, and wherever the lead horse stopped, they too would follow suit and stop. It's a herd mentality. I demonstrated at half speed by tying one horse at the end of the street on a horse trailer, blocking off the intersection with the horse trailer and truck. When the horses ran down the street, I stood and waved my hands with the cowboy hat in the air, directing them to the other horse, and sure enough, they stopped. The cops allowed us to film and I had saved that shoot.

The horses had on Borium horse shoes, which added traction, so they could run on the asphalt. We got the shot, but at the very end, one of the horses actually skidded a little bit to the side, cutting across the rubber mat we had in place and almost cut through the thick power cable from the generator. Almost had BBQ horse (The horse was fine, it was the last shot, and everything worked).

So, this cop who showed up remembered me and said, "You that crazy cowboy with the horses on Broadway!" I said, "True that, my man." He said, "Ok. It's all good here then. You got this." Now, this is a multi-million dollar shoot, so to lose all the extras, actors, limos, government motorcade vehicles and all of the people dressed in tuxedos and opera gear would have been an expensive loss so I got another "Sorry" and "thank you Andre!"

It was the next day that I was supposed to do a scene with my dog where we sniffed out the bomb in one of the music cases in the music room. At lunch time, the fat ass lady from the animal company rudely said to one of her trainers, "Have you seen the other shepherds?" which her loser trainer replied, "Yeah, they ain't shit." It took all I had to keep from getting up and crashing a folding chair over their heads like a pro-wrestling ring. I said, "Your time will come."

The second unit team and director asked me if I would use one of her shepherds for that scene. I said, "Ok, but Shepherd Rescue gets the credit, and in the final scene tomorrow, in front of the opera house when the big event takes place, only our dogs work." They agreed. I have nothing bad to say about other people's dogs.

Next day rolled around. We are about to film the final scene where the bomb is going to go off in the opera house. By the way I had great talks with Steve Carell. What a talented, wonderful, humble man he is; hope to work with him again. It was after lunch and we were waiting with our walkies to be called to the front of the Disney Concert Hall, as all the people would be pouring in and the dogs were needed. I was promised that my dogs would be used for the scene, so I was ready and had them in my truck when I got the call.

It was then that I noticed her red pickup racing to the front of the building and pulling out her German shepherds. I had had enough. I walked up to the front where she was standing with her dog and a smug look. But she didn't have a uniform. She wasn't there as a bomb squad cop. That was not the deal. So, in front of 120 people on the corner of 1ˢᵗ and Broadway, I said, "Hell, no! It ain't gonna happen. It's our dogs or no dogs; or her fat ass can get into my uniform and play the role" (which I knew she couldn't do). I unclipped my gun belt and holster, threw it on the ground and looked at her because she knew what she had done. I said, "Go ahead. Squeeze your fat ass into that and play the role." You have to understand that I was fighting for all those German Shepherds who didn't have homes, who's faces had been burned by acid by maniacs, who had cut up paws, etc. It was my purpose, calling and cause, and I assure you that I would have shut down the shoot in 5 min. I was ready with the SAG hotline, SPCA and my friend who worked for the county that told me to film.

They would have lost their finale and last day. I said, "Don't anybody even think about approaching me and talking to me about this. You are done." I started to walk away and got ready to shut it down when I heard a voice from the distance, "ANDRE YOU WON! YOU WON! LOOK! LOOK!" I looked up the street and I saw the little pickup truck with the dogs and the fat ass lady peeling away. The director Peter was calling me...we had won one for German Shepherd Rescue and all the dogs that deserved a chance.

Eventually, I had to put Goldie down. We, vets included, forgot to realize that even though, without pads, her skin grew back on the bottom of her feet, there was only bone with a thin layer of skin to concrete and nothing the vet or I tried had worked. The only other option was foot grafts for $10,000 and the vet told me that skin grafts only work if they are not on the bottom of your feet. It would have been cruel to not put her to sleep; the nerve endings on the bottom of her feet were cut off and she would run herself bloody.

I adopted "Wolfgang," or "Wolf" for short, a black German shepherd who had somebody throw acid on his head which fried his whole face. He had been guarding a property and the people who he barked at got busted. They came back and thanked him with acid. I took him on gladly. After Goldie, I asked them to give me their worst case.

The next weekend, I went back to Shep Rescue and a van pulled up in front. It was Saturday, and everyone was there to adopt. This magnificent creature jumped out. He was huge, but he moved like a smaller Shepherd and almost looked like a lion. Everyone wanted this dog. Everyone asked, "What is it? What is it? And the word "King Shepherd" came out. I have had shepherds since I was 5 years old and had the original bloodline descendent from the Hollywood movie star dog, Rin Tin Tin, the Hero German Shepherd, but I had never seen anything like this. Everyone wanted Konig, which means "King" in German.

At that point, there was such a frenzy, but the Shep Rescue people said, "Wait! Wait everybody! First offer goes to Andre!" For taking the least, I got the two best. Konig was my movie dog. I would use him on multiple TV shows and on the movie *Hop*. We played the K9 cowboy act. It was hilarious because we were in the middle of Downtown LA and it was ridiculously hot and muggy, and the whole production company was crowded for space. For the entire production, they took over one of those outdoor parking lots that you pay for, but still, space was really tight and there were hundreds of people onset; there still wasn't enough room for trailers and everything. It was one of the hottest days in summer and I had asked them where I should put my dog.

I figured they would give me a little trailer or a cool corner of the theatre for my dog. I came to find out that in the middle of this tight parking lot was a red tent that was probably 25 feet by 25 feet easily, with fake grass carpeting, its own benches and a generator with a giant tube blowing cold air into the tent. I asked, "Who is this all for?" They replied, "It's for you and Konig." Well, for the first time, I wasn't too upset with Union and SAG. However, it was so hot that I felt bad for the extras and other production crew who were sitting out there, trying to find shade somewhere as they were brought in and out the theatre all day.

I told people to grab a cold drink and follow me, and started bringing people into the tent to sit down and cool off. They'd ask, "What is this place?!" and I said, "It's for my dog, Konig." Truly Konig, the King Shepherd, had got his own onset palace and was treated better than the humans. At one point, I was in front of the theatre when there was a lot of people lined up and walking by me. While Konig was very nice to everyone, he was very alert. This fast-walking African American lady tried to pass and he growled, barked and backed her up against the wall and kept barking at her between sitting and looking at me.

One of the crew said, "Your K9 is trained for drug sniffing too? That's awesome!" What I didn't know, and had later found out, was that the lady was on drugs and had them on her. I asked the Shep Rescue where Konig had come from. When they told me Stockton, California, I tried to research where he might have come from. Stockton is one of the top places for sheriffs' K9 training facilities in California. He must have been owned by a Sheriff because this dog came totally trained and well-quipped. He was really a miracle dog.

I brought him to use on Desperate Housewives. That day, I played the role of a blind man and worked with Eva Longoria; when she saw Konig, she wanted to play with him and take pictures. It had pissed off the whole set for the delay that was caused, but it was fine with me. At the end of the day, when we were wrapping up, I had Konig next to me between a parking lot curb and my car.

The whole parking lot was empty, so you could have easily went around me, but believe it or not, a grip came up behind us with a leather glove and slapped Konig on the back of his head. This guy was clearly an asshole. Konig did what he was supposed to, and I encouraged it, to which the grip backed away a few feet and said, "You're lucky your dog didn't bite me, or I would have stabbed him!" I put my dog back in the car, took off my shirt and said, "What did you say? The dog's put away and it's just you and me now. Bring your knife over here you son of a bitch. And when I'm done with you, you're gonna look awfully stupid with that knife sticking out of your ass!" That shit enrages me, especially after what had happened to Goldie because of a maniac with a knife.

This guy had no idea the fuse he lit. I noticed him get quiet and think about it for a minute. I started to walk towards him. He started to walk away. Smartest decision of his life. I had with self-defence, Krav Maga, and pulling knives out of people's hands and got no problem taking a minor cut for it. But once I get it, the opposite attacker is in a lot of trouble. After the whole scene, a couple of electricians had kind of clapped and said, "We saw it! We saw all of it! What is that dick's problem?!" I said, "Well, the problem is he almost had a knife sticking out of his ass." They laughed. Hollywood is full of asshole idiots.

I had worked on a show called "Dirty Sexy Money" because all money is dirty; nothing sexy about it...only what it can buy, I suppose, if money is your god. Anyway, I had known Donald Sutherland from the Fox lot and from the movie *MASH*, but this was the first time really working with him. I played the casino pit manager. The scene was supposed to be in an extremely expensive luxury casino yacht; a super high stakes poker game of which Donald Sutherland was playing in. This was on the Paramount lot, and I didn't much care for working with Donald. Kiefer I liked working with.

Working with Donald was a pain in the ass. He liked the set so freezing cold that you could hang meat in there. You could almost see your own breath, which was no matter for Donald, who would have an oversized puffy down parka on. His quirk was that when they rolled the scene, he would take off the jacket and his shoes, and as soon as the scene stopped, they would run his jacket back to him and his shoe valet, the magic slipper fairy, would run over and put the shoes back on to Donoldrella. It was really uncomfortable to watch because this guy's whole job was running back Donald's shoes and putting them on his feet and putting his jackie on him.

The only thing I could figure was that maybe, just like when you drive a car at night and you get sleepy, if you take your shoes off, you are more alert. I don't quite understand the cold room thing. Some sort of a method acting? Acted like a queen as far as I'm concerned. That's why we called him Prima- Donald. Anyway. Thanks for the memories. Moving on, new deal.

Kiefer was cool, and I enjoyed working with him. I like his work from *The Lost Boys* and *Young Guns*. Congratulations on inheriting your career. I worked for a great director named Frank Borin, who I did a TV show pilot called *Santa Cruz*, a Simon Cowell production (*American Idol*), who I don't much care for either. If I were ever on the show and he disrespected me, the name of the show would be "American Knockout". Simon, you know you go overboard and need some grounding, as in a dirt nap.

Frank had called me because he had a new directing partner named Kiefer Sutherland. They were going into the music business together and had done a music video for a band called *Billy Boy on Poison*. Now, I don't know what happened to the band, but with a name like that, they either didn't get too far or are in Rehab.

The shoot took place at the Inglewood Forum, and the gag was that Billy Boy or Billy Boys, whatever they are, broke into the forum and found a whole set of musical equipment, all of which was conveniently there and plugged in, and they decided to jam, not realizing that they set off the silent alarm. That's when L.A.P.D. and I roll in. Kiefer had me lead the cops, as I was stunt coordinator and lead stuntman cop, and tell them what to do as the band was jamming. I ran in, guns drawn, flashlights on, yelling at the band, "Cease and get on the ground!" Now, if you ever broke into anywhere in Inglewood and the police show up, that's how it would be. Now, I have this idiot Australian actor who I had already taken a major role away from in the *Tears of Christ* movie at Universal as Praetorian Roman squad leader. He was still bitter and trying to tell me how cops would never act that way.

He and the other cops were standing around, doing nothing, so Kiefer yelled, "Cut! Cut! Cut! What's wrong with you guys?! This is Inglewood, California. Cops would come storming in here!" at which point he said, "Andre. You did a great job. Now everyone, do the same!" I shined my flashlight into the wanna-be Jason Statham's eye and laughed at him. No wonder I took the role away from him. This guy thought he'd be the next Russell Crowe, but he was acting like Russell Ho, coming into *my* town, and trying to tell me how the police would arrest you here. I, of all people, should know both sides.

After that scene, I was to get into the police car and do the stunt driving. I had done a few rehearsals and was supposed to come sliding in at a 180 degree turn as fast as I could, through the parking lot, lock it up sideways and stop inches before the curb in perfect place, right into B camera. I suggested the camera man not be standing there, but they were confident in my skills and insisted he stay there.

As I'm about to go, I see the passenger door open, and Kiefer pops his head inside and asks, "Mind if I go for a ride?" He wanted to go along for the stunt. I said, "You have nothing to worry about. I'll drive extra crazy and take many risks." He thought about it, shoved his camera man in the front seat and he jumped in the back, yelling, "Let's Roll!" It's not common for a director to do that.

He actually asked me if I could drive outside into the streets of Inglewood in the cop car to get some footage. He had found the right guy. I was dressed like L.A.P.D. and had a cop car, so naturally, I took the liberty of doing what every one of you would want to do. I lit up the cherries, turned on the sirens and started racing around the LA forum on the streets of Inglewood, as if we were on a 911 call, on the way to make an arrest. I was running through intersections, passing in the centre divider and getting sideways every chance I got. People were getting the heck out of my way and drug dealers and crackheads were jumping for cover. I was having too much fun, and was probably starting to freak out

Kiefer a little bit. I must have been crazier than the people on the streets.

He then asked if we could head back. We came hauling ass back into the driveway, catching a little air. He asked if I could check the brakes, so I slammed on the emergency brake, got the car sideways, did a few donuts in the parking lot to make noise and headed for the curve. I Slid into it sideways, locked it up, guns drawn and raided the forum. Great shot, and I got extra money for it. It was fun working with you Kiefer. Hope to work with you again.

At the end of the shoot, when I was collecting my cash, they gave me an extra envelope of cash. Do you know that Russel Ho had the nerve to come up to me and complain about my extra money? I said to him, "Do you need me to make your reservations?" When he asked for what, I got in his face and said, "For the beat down motel, 'cause you're about to check in. The only problem is, when you check in, you check out, and you don't remember your stay. Now get out of my way and shut up and don't ever talk to me again. You're all in my Kool-Aid and you don't even know the flava," as we say in the hood. His career is somewhere with Billy Boy on Poison.

Working with Enrique Iglesias was a pleasure. Enrique was a gentleman, and very talented. His father must have raised him right, and he wasn't like most singing stars who had an attitude, but he had as much right, if not more to be that way, I suppose. He had 95% more talent than anyone at singing. But of course, he is Julio Iglesias's son.

It was another extremely hot day, and I was to be stunt coordinator, stuntman, second unit director and play a fireman. This was the era where in almost every music video Enrique was making, he was either bleeding, on the ground getting shot or crying. As I was rigging the crashed car, pulling him out of the wreck while he was singing on the stretcher and being whisked away by the ambulance, I thought, "Enough with the crying on the stretcher, on the ground bleeding and singing. Can we move on to some happier videos, Enrique?"

He had his Latin entourage around him and I had the full fireman's uniform on, including fireproof boots that came up almost to my waist, a huge thick fireproof jacket and the helmet. They wanted the complete look. Enrique, God bless you, I think it's great that you love your fans enough to shoot 2 versions of the same video in English and in Spanish; but man, it was a long, hot day. At one point, I started to feel dizzy and couldn't figure out why. I had so much gear on that it didn't allow for my pores to breathe; not to mention, the gear isn't meant to be worn for 12 hours straight. Clearly, this was a non-union shoot, but we got through the day. We even had real paramedics on set working in the scene. When one of them asked me, "Where are you out of?" I said, "L.A." Later that day, I figured out after they were calling me "Sir," that they meant "What fire station." They thought I was the real deal (Fire Captain) because they were. I didn't want burst their bubble, so I let it go.

At the end of the day, I noticed that Enrique was speaking Spanish with his entourage. They kept pointing over at me, and one of the guys came over with Enrique and said, "Enrique would like to personally thank you, on behalf of him, his family and his fans for all that you do and did." He wanted to take a picture with me, so I guess he thought the same thing that the paramedics thought, and I did what most men would do in Hollywood. I had to tell him, "Gracias! De Nada! El Gusto es Mio!" (English translation: Thank you! You're welcome, the pleasure is mine.)

I was also working on set back at Sony/MGM, where I played a director of photography for a new TV show at that time called *Party of Five*. I met a girl on set who was very talented, very humble and had amazing charisma and a peaceful presence about her. I walked over at the end of the day and found that it was one of her first days working and filming. I said, "Young lady, I just want to tell you that I believe that you will be an A list star, and you have a great spirit." She smiled at me and said, "I was just going to tell you the same." Her name is Jennifer Love Hewitt. On sets, her nickname is "Love," which was pretty cool. She is a great actress and did a music video with Enrique called "Hero," featuring Mickey Rourke; I don't know if she's who got Enrique onto the crying.

I worked with so many people in the industry, but I call it like I see it. I worked in a music video with Beyoncé. And I gotta tell you, it was a negative experience. At the end of the day, after working with her all day, I asked for a picture. Her family and she just declined in a very rude manner with a bad attitude. Maybe it was the cross I had on my neck, it must have had a vampire effect on her.

Since you didn't want to take a picture, here is a picture that captures the mood of that day. But that's ok, because I don't appreciate her music videos that encourage the burning of our police cars and endorsing riot scenes among the African Americans. After her Superbowl appearance, representing the BLM (Black Lives Matter) in her Black Panther outfit, I don't appreciate the Dallas Police officers that were murdered due to the encouragement of violence through her so-called music. I also don't like music videos of Lil Wayne burning the American flag and stomping on it, or the NFL players disrespecting our National Anthem by not standing, a new trend of higher disrespect and dissention among our Nation, thanks to the Obama administration, the UN and BLM. Jesus died for all and said all lives matter, meaning all colours, so the BLM stands for Black Lies don't Matter.

In Serbia we were enslaved and oppressed by the Ottoman Empire, aka Islam, for over 500 years, then after that, by the Nazis, and afterwards by the communists. So, do I begin my oppression list? No. Everyone has to take responsibility for their own life and actions, and we can become anything we want in America; it just requires action and hard work. But I assure you from my family's history, as well as global history, that if we allow our freedoms and our first amendment (the right to speak out over anything) to be taken and destroyed, without the 2nd Amendment, you will never have a right to the 1st, and only the government wins. Just ask all the Native Americans who were slaughtered once they handed in their weapons, as Geronimo, the Great American War Chief said at the end of his life, "I should have never surrendered. I should have fought until I was the last man alive."

History proves that 280 million people were murdered by communism once they were disarmed. All of you who are not supporting America, you will not like the outcome of communism and socialism, and it is coming our way if we don't unite as the United States of America. I love my Country, Military and law enforcement, and I support them in every way. I believe that anybody who makes millions in Hollywood, under the protection and freedom that our United States Military provides them, should either support them or move out of America. I will personally help you pack.

After all of the things that have happened to me, I decided to do a show to respect and honour all the real stuntmen, daredevils and heroes around the world; not all of the GoPro jockey junkies that have been splatting on the sides of rocks in Europe and in different drop zones, and endangering other people's lives, nor the wanna-be, green-screen, wire-work, fake stuntmen. I created a show called "Adrenaline Man," and I am the Adrenaline Man. I signed a deal with 3 East Coast producers for the letter of intent from ABC and a purchase order. As executive producers, it was their obligation to raise the money at 75% ownership of the show, and me, doing all the daredevil stunts and risking my life for 25%; but I was ok with that for God, Family and County. What I wasn't ok with was their bullshit phone call at the end of a couple of months after we signed the contract, asking me if I could raise the money. After spending almost half a million dollars on training, trademarks, websites, product line and much more, these East Coast buffoons were more idiotic than Robert De Niro and his stand against Trump.

During that time, these 3 chowder-head, wanna-be "Goodfellas" had burned Discovery Channel on an offer because they thought ABC was bigger. After finding out about the money, and them saying that they would gladly fly out to receive the check for doing nothing, I kindly explained to them about the geography of the United States of America and how lucky they were that I didn't live on the East Coast and accidently show up at their front door to give them a Brooklyn hickey. A Brooklyn hickey is when you open a man's mouth on the edge of the curb, with their teeth on the cement, and "accidently" stomp on the back of their heads. But eh, one too many Martin Scorsese movies I must have seen. What I wanted to do to them would have been tame in comparison to the movie *Raging Bull* and *Casino*.

Basically, I told them never to call me or bother me again or they may receive a dead fish wrapped in a newspaper to their front door or find a horse's head in their bed one night. That's Sicilian for "we got no deal, consider yourself lucky".

I proceeded to call ABC broadcasting myself, only to speak with a rude President Geri Wang, who had a bad attitude; she will find out how very wang she was to treat me that way. I immediately decided to go back to Discovery channel but remembered that they were very interested in making the deal, but were burned by the 3 stooges of production, my ex partners on the East Coast. So, I went to the top, Elliot Wagner, CEO and Global President for Discovery Channel, nothing less.

I remember tracking his number down and my wife looking at me in a dirt parking lot in California saying, "You really think you can get a hold of him personally?" I prayed, I called and 2 rings later, Elliot Wagner answered the phone. Just like at Universal Pictures where the president picked up the phone, Elliot said he came back in to retrieve something out of his office, his secretary wasn't in, and so he had to answer the phone. Tell me there's no God. He remembered hearing about me and being excited about the show and wondered why we burned and disrespected Discovery. I simply explained the 3 losers who should have snapped the Prozac in half before making any phone calls to Discovery, and what complete imbeciles they were. Elliot laughed, and we started to rebuild our relationship and clear the good name of the *Adrenaline Man*.

We were off and running again. He then told me to call 2 of his main broadcasting and sales associates for New York and the US, to whom he had highly recommended me. Upon calling them, they too remembered me and asked me what happened. I explained to them the frauds of New York, apologized on their behalf and said that I am a man of my word and I do what I say, and I say what I do. I immediately shot them over the paperwork and contracts and they received it in good faith. I was able to soil the bad names of the prior producers, rendering them useless to ever do business with ABC, Discovery and many more major channels.

I got a deal with Discovery Communications, but during that time I got called into the office of United Artists, Roma Downey and Mark Burnett's, of *Survivor* fame. Roma and Mark are wonderful people and are doing great things. The only problem is that they don't have a lot of great people working under them all the time. As I walked in, they said,

"Would you be willing to do something to promote Adrenaline Man?" I told them sure. They said, "We are looking for 6 near death experiences, and we have put out a global casting call for millions of people." But here was the deal. It couldn't have been a random act of luck that got you though this near-death experience. It had to be a higher power that clearly saved your life; God.

They had interviewed a lot of people, including a guy named Jeb "I got a bad attitude and a stick up my butt" Corliss. Jeb had been showing off in Africa, doing his wingsuiting, and had taken the name "The Bird Man," which was originally the nickname and call sign of my friend and wingsuit mentor, world champion wingsuiter Dave Barlia's. Dave is, and always will be, the original "Bird Man," so we will call Jeb the "Bird Brain," as he has such a pompous attitude and prides himself on treating people like shit. His claim to fame was a crash into some rocks, due to his own fault, and living through it. His name could have been "Bird Shit on the Rocks". I have seen him mistreating people at Perris drop zone, including Roberta Mancini, who he was dating. We used to all jump out of the same plane a lot. But Mark Burnett and Roma Downey's production company said that he had a bad attitude and was an egomaniac, which I thought was polite, considering he's way worse than that, and so they did not use him. "We need humble," they said. So, I told them my story and had many more. They picked the car-wreck story of my epic, high-speed tumble in a little convertible.

They came to my house and were overwhelmed by the documentary and info that they filmed on me, with enough footage for almost 12 hours. Everything from training in my personal gym, to live samurai sword demo and hours of interviewing. Roma Downey was at her house nearby, and Wendy, the executive producer, was on her computer with Roma the whole time, which I didn't know until later. My episode aired on TLC, the sister channel to Discovery, and was the highest rated episode. Discovery had looked up the ratings, though TLC had tried to bury the show because they had another stupid show called *Long Island*

Medium (she looked more like a large to me). Sometimes you talk about God, and people can't take it, especially in Hollywood. So, my job as the *Adrenaline Man* is to show that I should have been dead many times, but by the Grace of God only, I am still alive to tell the story and give Him the Glory.

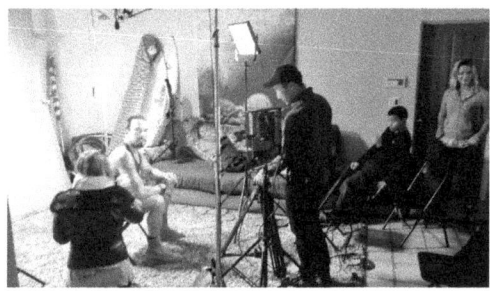 

Mark and Roma were amazing and I was saddened to see that they lived close, by but their producers had offered me nothing. They even used my house for free to film another episode of *Answered Prayers,* but I know that the producers had gotten fired for stealing the money that they were supposed to give out per diem to the people and for the locations. In Hollywood, it's called petty cash, and it's to be used for whatever necessary expenses come along for production. A lot of the time, tens of thousands of dollars accidentally evaporate into producer's pockets so I call it "petty theft." And you wonder why they get fired, disappear and have to look for new jobs.

It doesn't leave you with a good feeling. I should have you know, Mark and Roma, you guys are great, but Allyson and Wendy are a mess; they lied to me and never paid me a cent after I line-produced and put that whole episode together. I was promised that they would work with me on *Adrenaline Man.* Ha! Yeah, sure.

I realized that we had a timeline issue with Discovery and *Adrenaline Man,* so I had to think fast, as the condition of the world was deteriorating. Originally, we were supposed to do many global episode locations, but I found travel to be unsafe for all crew. For example, it was no longer an option to fly to Venezuela to film the world's highest waterfall jump while their country was in the state of collapse, and they were eating their flamingos and zoo animals. Due to Obama's fake proxy war, Dubai towers and Middle East was also unsafe. All of Europe was invaded by fake Muslim, so-called Syrian rape-u-gees, so it was not safe for us to film in Italy, France, Spain, Germany, UK or Sweden.

Obama's administration had opened our borders and let in millions of Middle Eastern and global terrorists, South American drug cartel, MS13, and was utilizing and turning African Americans into puppets for the DNC and for Communism. America was not safe anymore; something had to happen.

I remember sitting and watching an episode of Alex Jones and hearing that my mentor and friend, James Cameron, had moved to New Zealand to film more Avatar and that the globalists and elites who had money were moving there as well. I quickly did my research on NZ and not only did I find that it was safe with non-GMO foods, but had unbelievable scenery, with caverns and caves to explore, great white sharks galore, killer whales to swim with, amazing skydiving and Peter Jackson had wrapped up *Lord of the Rings* there.

NZ was up and coming as far as movie and film production, and was known as the "Adrenaline Capital of the World" with minimal unions or lawsuits. In other words, their policy is that if you are stupid enough to jump off a cliff, a bridge or get eaten while outside of a cage in great white shark infested waters, it's not our fault or problem and you can't sue us. Perfect! Not to mention James Cameron's haunting words, "I will never raise my children in this America." I have to agree with that.

Looking at the country of New Zealand, with it's population of 5 million people, compared to the size of the state of California, and it's 15 million in LA alone, I said to myself, "Self, you don't gotta ask me twice." In my tradition of taking my time and not making hasty decisions, I said, "I'm out of here." I remember selling my truck, my stuff and everything that I ever dreamed of, from my horses, my 3 German Shepherds, to all the desires of my heart. I packed 2 suitcases, a pair of shorts, a leather Harley jacket and left with a 3-month return flight ticket.

I wanted to get a longer-term Visa, and called the NZ embassy in California, but some libtard, Kiwi, Santa Monica Embassy guy told me, "You can't just do that. You have to send me your passports and we will let you know in a few months." So, I shrugged my shoulders, rubbed my eye with my middle finger (signifying universal gorilla language to stuff it) and hung up the phone. That voice was talking to me again and told me "Get out of America. Judgement day is coming." This book was mostly written and completed before President Trump was elected. You are going to hear about the mess…the dirty secrets of the DNC, the UN globalists, the Clintons, the Obama's, and much more.

First of all, I will have you know that I am a Trump supporter. Anyone who says that they love America, but hate Trump are either uninformed libtards and morons, or un-American traitors, as Trump stands for God,

Family, Country, our Military and our Police, who have, over the last 8 years, been murdered in our streets and around the world due to the Obama administration and sick people in charge.

But first, let's pay a little visit to Dorothy. Dorothy, a NY book agent, promised me a six-figure advance for my book "within 90 days". I thought Hollywood was all BS, but the editing and publishing world is just as bad, if not worse. Not only did Dorothy not deliver, but also lied constantly. At one point, when Trump got elected, she said to me, and I quote, "I am moving to Cuba now and I can't wait for that asshole to be assassinated." Not something you want to hear from your agent.

Now she had been discussing my story with a group called the Weinsteins. Yes, those Weinsteins. The offer was that they would be interested in publishing my book, but all the stories, movie rights and royalties would go to them. Wow. They learned how to rape people early didn't they? I had a bad feeling about the Swinesteins and wanted nothing to do with them. Amazing how your instincts can be right, and you better listen to them when they are loud and clear. These same Weinsteins are the jerks, paedophiles, and perverts who are being sued by thousands of people, and busted open the whole Hollywood paedophile, homosexual and baby blood drinking bastard ring that they are. So, at that point, there wasn't much I could do with Dorothy since she is a traitorous scumbag like the rest of them. But I will tell you this, if I find any of my stories re-written by ghost writers, and it traces back to Dorothy, Cuba will not be big enough for her to hide from me or God.

New Zealand is the most beautiful country I have been to, the safest, and still has natural and healthy foods. However, I was surprised to find out that the people here are even more liberal than California, if that is even possible; and I don't mean that as a good thing. They are not only uninformed, but are bottle fed CNN (Commie News Network), and sometimes worse. How can you take over a country and sell it over to China and the UN, if they find out that a real American President,

Commander in Chief Donald Trump, has been exposing the globalists around the world? You have to feed the people mainstream propaganda and keep them blinded.

I am shocked at everything I am watching happen all around the world, from the fake war in Syria that Obama started to flood Europe with rape-u-gees, to Merkel, who is a German Nazi UN shell, as well as the Canadian Trudeau, who is also a UN Muslim shill. But it sure does prove that God is real, and the book of Revelation is coming true. We are entering the last years and the battle of Armageddon; the Bible calls the UN the *One World Government.* Boy are they knocking themselves out to rape, lute, kill and create manmade weather storms, floods, disease, cancer, fake news and so much more.

All that is happening is as my Grandma had taught me; it's Communism and Socialism 101. I am watching it all happen. First provide the problem, then provide the solution by disarming the people mentally, physically and spiritually, and then you can take them over. I am in disbelief to see how many people around the world are still putting up with all of this BS. How can you not see that all of this is a premeditated set-up to thin the herd, or if you don't know what that means, wipe out much of the population by using racial warfare, genocide and financial collapses all around the world. Is this a coincidence? If you believe that it is, you might as well put this book down because you won't like the truth and it won't be a happy ending. But I will keep it straight because I am one of the few that still has the real balls to tell you the truth and not what you want to hear. The UN libtard lying media puts you in a deadly situation that they benefit from.

Fast forward to March 18, 2018, my birthday. I have made it to my promise land after weeding out so many negative people, witches, hackers and apostate phony churches (as the Bible said would be in the last days). As far as the eye can see, here are rolling green hills, lakes, cattle, ducks, geese, turkeys, pheasant, natural drop zones, forests, wild bush, wild pigs, deer, goats, sheep… a hunter and survivalist's paradise; right where you would want to be as you are reading this chapter and getting freaked out by my words. Sorry, but I keep it real. You all better have some bags of rice, fresh water, topped off gas tanks, some way to protect yourself and invest in precious metals. My 2 favorites are gold and lead.

What's going to happen since China and Russia are hoarding all of the gold and they came up with a one-world monetary system together- there is that Bible again talking about the *One-World Monetary System*? God, God is right. So, when they shut off the internet and the power grids, which they will do, you better have something besides a piece of plastic and dead ipads and cell phones in your hand while you are being bum rushed by

Harry Madera
BARRY SOTERO AKA BARRACK AND MICHELLE OBAMA AKA MICHEAL LAVAUGHAN ROBINSON IN THEIR EARLY DAYS...

Malia and Sasha Obama's
Real parents Marty and Anita Blanchard Nesbitt

criminals, looters, rioters and maniacs from undeveloped countries that the UN, in their own PC way, told you are "alright". By the way, in case I didn't mention it before, PC stands for Political Corruptness, as I am watching FBI James Comey, and every mayor of every Sanctuary, or what I call Skanktuary, city getting busted for voter fraud, paedophilia, stealing hundreds of billions from America from the DNC and the republicans we thought we could count on, who have turned into traitors, or as we call them, Rinos. The truth is out. Barack Obama, aka Barry Soetoro, is not only a liar, but a fraud, a Muslim, a globalist, a communist... oh, and he was born in Hawaii, as in Hawaii, *Kenya*. He is not only responsible for this fake Syrian war, but also for the Benghazi murders because our Ambassador found out that he and Hillary Clinton have sold our US Military weapons to ISIS (who he is the founder of), lost 2 full-size intercontinental ballistic missiles on his watch and gave 150 billion dollars to our arch enemy, Iran. The list is so long, we would cover this whole book with his crimes. He just recently visited New Zealand to hide because President Trump has remodelled Guantanamo Bay, and has a room for him and Michelle Obama, aka Michelle LaVaughn Robinson, who was born a man and still has Mr. Johnson in his front pocket, as we saw that fly out on the Ellen Degenerate show (she also got a medal of honour for nothing but being gay).

Five thousand arrest warrants have been put out and a special platoon of bad ass Marine Corp, run by one of my favorite people, the one and only General Mad Dog Mattis aka *Chaos*. As I am writing this, another huge Military Hercules airplane flew overhead, which is really strange considering they really don't have an Airforce in NZ. So, it's just our Communist friends from China, who bought this place from the previous government in 2014. That is why we moved out to farmland. Because for 3 years, I saw tens of thousands of Chinese flooding into the country of NZ, and they got anything and everything they wanted. I have never seen a Bentley SUV with a learners permit on it, and people who can't even back up their lime green Lamborghini, but "don't worry" they say, as I am watching them purchase all of Auckland, all of the dairies, getting Residency, and even for an American, what I am about to say is completely insane.

Here we are, a country who bitches about the fake crisis actors and set-up school shootings, and talks about our American firearms, when Auckland is the highest firearm capital on this planet. Do you know why? Because the Kiwis are giving the Chinese E and C category firearm permits, and they are buying them up in the cartloads. An E-Cat is a Military and a C-Cat is a Collectable, including fully automatic machine guns, sub machine guns with thousands of rounds of ammo as long as the Chinese promise not to shoot them. Laughable! I don't know how you say this in Chinese, but in English it would be "Mee Blake Mai Plomise" and they break their promise every day on farmland, in groups of 20-30 and nothing happens. They don't get their license revoked or get deported. Really? I was born at night but not last night. Shit's getting hot all over the world.

The great thing about President Trump is that he's putting his boot in everyone's ass all around the world, exposing mass corruptions, murderers, fake media, lying libtards and he's going after people, arresting them, cutting off their funds, deporting them and doing all the normal stuff all of our real American Presidents have done for decades, except for Barry. And our sick Secretary of State, Hillary Clinton. This bitch stole 200 thousand dollars of artwork and furniture from the White House when her sexual predator, that should be at the end of a rope with her, got caught getting a BJ by some fat libtard chick and leaving a mess on her dress. They made Killary, as I call her, give it back. Oh, by the way her personal body count, not including fake wars and Benghazi, is over 50 people. I guess people meet her and just feel like killing themselves. It's amazing, one guy even shot himself in the back of his own head 2 times. Wow! You wanna talk about an amazing shooter. Her and Billy Bob have been on the hook in Arkansas for fake land scams, under the table cocaine deals, not to mention getting paid by the Muslims in the Croatian Bosnian War, who's butts us Serbians were kicking in a well-deserved way in a private war until Bill got caught with his pants down and decided to take the heat off of him by screaming "Genocide" helping the wrong side out and bombing the Christian Serbians hospitals, schools, and metropolitan city of Belgrade, enabling Islam to keep growing terrorist camps in the former Yugoslavia . Thanks a lot asshole. There is a special place for you and Hillary in Hell. And there ain't gonna be no 72 virgins there, even if you are white-trash, Muslim sell-outs. Hillary is hiding in India as we speak, and all of her emails have been exposed; everything, from putting hits out on people, to selling Uranium to the Russians. It's all there in Black and White.

Or should I say in Black and Black, as I am watching the BLM Black Libtard Movement aka Black Panther Commies put out violent hate movies and incite that scumbag murderer Mugabe and his gang slaughtering white people and farmers in South Africa by the blacks. Not only is there no persecution, but it is encouraged. Excuse me but WHAT THE FUCK?! And the leader of the black Communist party in South Africa said this, and I quote, "If the whites are going to run away to a racist country like Australia, they can at least leave the keys to their house and tractors behind." These bitches aren't even smart enough to change the locks and get the tractors started...I would just tell all the whites to get out and do a nice carpet bombing campaign, courtesy of the US Marine Corps and the Australian Forces. White Genocide is the best kept secret and has gone worldwide. I can't even believe what I am seeing in America with black people saying, "You owe us your house and more compensation." The Irish were mistreated way worse in white slavery. In addition to that, biggest collectors of black slaves were the blacks themselves and the Muslims. The world has gone full tilt fucktard stupid mode and it is stuck on stupid till it's jarred loose by a good war and God's judgement.

As for the so-called Pope and his paedophile priests around the world, it may not be a known fact to you, but the first Christian crusade was started by the Templar Knights. They started the first banking system and went against Islamic terrorists of their day. And what did they get for their efforts? The pope in the 12th century talked to the Queen of France and they threw the Templar Knights a huge victory welcome back party where they hung them all, assumed the banking system, and have been promoting Islam and lies ever since. Even till this day. Well, Queen of France, how's that Muslim takeover looking for your country now? And the pope, who should be on a rope, is talking shit like, "We need a one world religion" ...Oh! The Bible is right again. And he even named it "Chris-lam" What the hell? First, you deny Christ... and if you think the Muslims are gonna give 50% of their cult and the Quran towards

Christianity, you are either a nut, a liar or both. This will not end well for anyone except the Christians; we know what the end of the book says, and God wins.

CHAPTER 11

THE TRUTH OF THE WORLD TODAY

WE ARE NEAR THE END OF THE BOOK, both mine and the Bible, so listen up and take some serious advice. Regardless of all the crazy stuff that I have seen throughout my whole life, if you would have told me some of these occurrences were going to take place, I wouldn't have believed most of it. Nonetheless, it's in our face, its reality and these are facts; not CNN lies.

As I am visiting New Zealand, and watching the world rapidly deteriorate, I get a great perspective on the rest of the world and come to the realization that Trump really is the right man to perform God's will. Trump just created peace between North and South Korea for the first time in 63 years; an amazing feat that should get the Nobel Peace Prize for this as everyone is calling for it.

I haven't concluded whether this is a good or bad thing since the Bible reads that a peace treaty will be made and then broken, resulting in the start of WWIII. However, that may very well apply to the Middle East, as we can clearly see Obama's Muslim brotherhood ties and fingerprints all over the Iran nuclear deal; which is about the stupidest deal I have ever heard of in my life. It's like approving a deal for a biker gang member to sell AK47s to another biker gang. Oh wait, he already did that when he

and Eric Holder sold AK47s to the Mexican Drug Cartel that murdered my friends and Border Patrol Agents. And now we're supposed to believe that it is in our better interest to apologize and give nuclear weapons and billions of dollars to our mortal enemy Iran, who has been burning our flag, killing our military, bombing Syria and Israel and chanting "Death to America"? This is also a country that states that as soon as they get nukes, they are going to wipe Israel off the face of the planet. And still, you don't want to be called an Islamophobe because it's the "religion of peace." Yeah sure.

Good for President Trump, General Mattis, Sarah Huckabee Sanders and all in charge who pulled the plug on the Iran (Nuclear Scam) deal. As I am writing this chapter, missiles are being exchanged between Iran and Israel. Israel has the right to defend itself without the UN making up more BS, such as "Jerusalem belongs to Palestine"; for the record, it never has and it never will. For over 4000 years, Jerusalem has belonged to the Jewish people. Even if you discount the Bible, which is all historic, you cannot discount Egyptian and Roman history, including the temple mount and the tomb of Jesus. How do you deny that a Jewish carpenter, who I call the Son of God, and others call a prophet, ever existed?

To top it all off, a massive volcano in Hawaii has gone active after globalists and the UN geoengineered a storm that flooded out Kauai. Good job by Laird Hamilton, famous Big wave surfer, for rescuing more people in the water again. He seems to be in the right place at the right time.

A volcano is going off and in California, my home state, I am shocked to watch all of the people there who haven't moved to Arizona, screaming for it to be a Sanctuary State. A Sanctuary for who? MS13? Islamic terrorists

around the world? Murderers? Rapists? Killers? Free loaders? They just arrested 1,600 people from the so-called Caravan, trying to flood into California from Mexico, and as they should; it's called an invasion. You try that in Mexico and let me know how it works out for you.

You would have thought that California would have had enough after the 55 fires that were set from 5,000 trillion watt lasers. But nope, they keep resisting America and our Patriots. At the same time, I am watching Patriotism on the rise. Even the morons in Hollywood can't stop our movement. Roseanne Barr's show had 18 million viewers the first week. Tim Allen's back on board with a cancelled ABC show *Last Man Standing*, representing America. And now, CBS has their hottest new show, *Seal Team*; it's funny to watch mega-marshmallow stars like George Clooney go down in flames and good to see my Patriot brothers and actors excel in Military and Police roles that glorify America and Patriotism. Great job Mark Wahlberg- God bless you for taking a stand.

Hawaii needs to be used as a landing strip in the middle of the Pacific Ocean for the Chinese army to invade and what land? You guessed it- Hi

California! Here's some more refugees for you; Chinese ones. You think this all was an accident to clear out California and Hawaii? There's a whole military city in Long Beach California housing Chinese soldiers and fake cargo ships, ready to open.

That explains why during the Obama administration LAX was closed to all international flights at night for over a week, the same week a huge intercontinental ballistic missile was tested over California.

So here we are in NZ, watching the same stupid libtard behavior that California had when Obama was in power. The airport was shut down for international flights for a week in NZ due to an "oil pipeline leak to the airport" Then, you a woman who has never had a job before, and has no experience in politics, running this country under "Labor Party" (which means Communist party) into the ground. All the while, she is hosting Barak Insane Obama and Hillary Kill-ton, wearing a bullet proof vest and charging $500 per Kiwi to talk shit about Trump and why she didn't win the election. But it doesn't matter because NZ has already been sold to China via Obama's good buddy, Mr. John Keys. God defend NZ…I hope so.

We are watching California ban Bibles. I can't believe that would even be said as a joke, but Jerry Moonbeam Brown has turned California, the Golden State, into a shit hole that's about to implode. But hey, that's all part of the grand plan, don't you know?

Iran's close buddies and allies are Russia, North Korea and China. Scary. But at least our allies, Canada, UK, France, Israel, Australia, Japan and South Korea are ready to go. And I kid you not… it's go time. I hope I have time to make appearances and do book signings. As they say in the hood, "the shits about to get real."

The fact that NZ was conveniently removed from Google Earth temporarily, many rich Chinese globalists and others are getting ready to hide down here. Even still, it is a good place to finish my book for now, as my beloved California and America will be blacked out and propelled into civil war and global warfare.

Just to make you all aware, WWIII does not mean the end of the world. Actually, what will happen is 1/3 of the world's population will be wiped out by famine, diseases, Agenda 21, manmade/natural disasters (some of God's wrath mixed in; shaken, not stirred) and then it will move onto what is known as Armageddon. That all starts and takes place with the beginning of the war in the Middle East. Oh, wait Iran and Israel! Middle East! Hey now.

If you still are not convinced by the world unraveling, let's hit this from another angle. Today's date is May 14, 2018, and America just opened the US embassy in Jerusalem, the capital of Israel. Now, we are watching this so-called religion of peace raid the borders of Israel, burning tires, throwing bombs, luting, rioting, all of which is basically an act of war. Many have died attacking Israel, and many will in the future.

There is a silent UN global gun grab going on. Communists and socialists always have to sugar coat everything before they stick it up your ass. It's called Gun Control. My friend Clint Eastwood has a saying, "I'm into gun control; If there is a gun in the room, I like to control it." Yes, we are here now. The UN tunnels under America have all been dug. The almost 50,000 fake FEMA camps are all over the US, with razor ribbon facing inward and fully stocked with non-English speaking, crazy, vial UN troops. The trains are ready to pull out with shekel's and chains in them, and yes, we have all seen the millions of black FEMA coffins that hold 4 bodies being trucked around America.

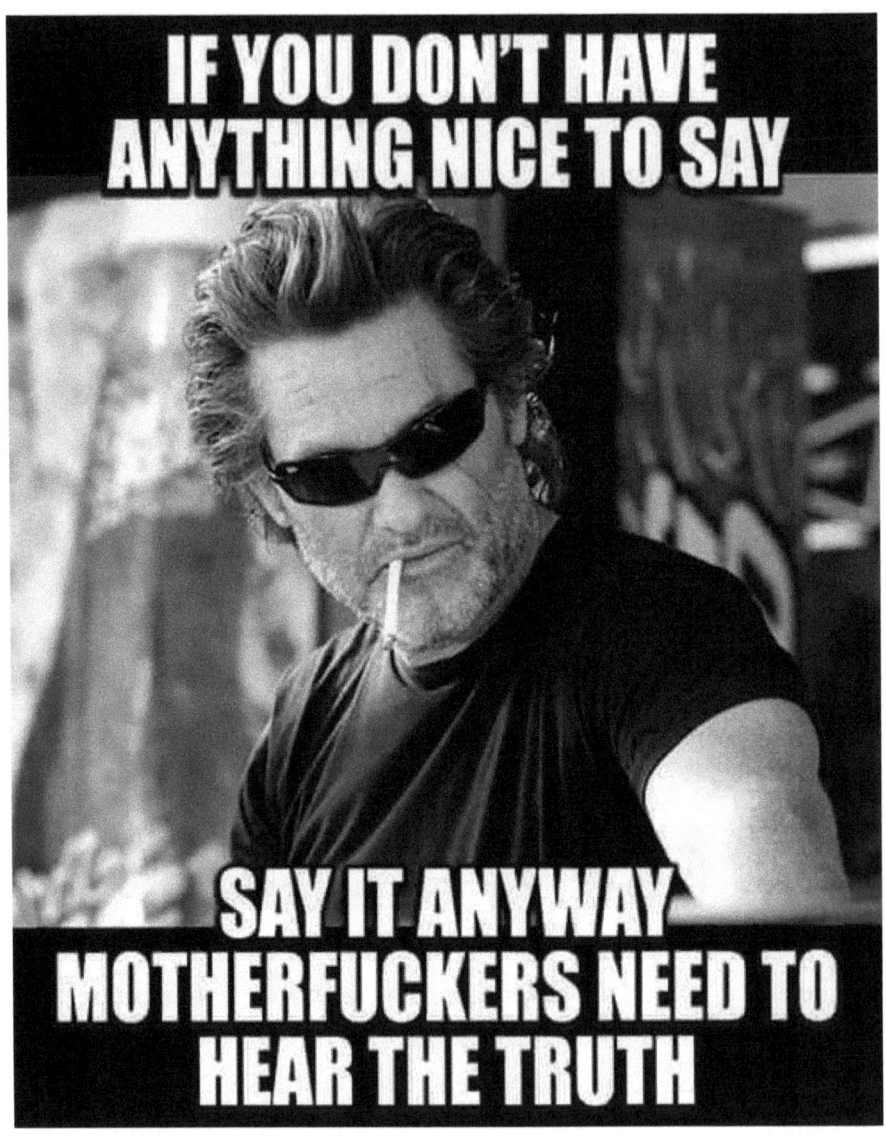

Just so you know, all the chemical trailing, chem bombing, weather manipulation, HAARP machines and EMF signals are not just for America. The one world government thinks they are going to take over the world and get all of us, but God, the only God, has other plans, and He has written them down in the book I speak of; Bible prophecy has never been wrong. Let me make something clear to you all- Allah, Mohammed, Buddha, Confucius, the Pope, Mary...none of them ever died for your sins, paid for them, raised the dead, healed the sick, cast out demons or has the most popular tourist attraction in the world where people wait for hours to see an empty tomb. Why? Because Jesus really did raise from the dead on the 3rd day and was seen walking around again by 500 credible witnesses. So, when you get to the crossroads of your life, which are you going to follow, the guy who is a pile of bones in a grave still or the guy named Jesus, the Son of God who actually rose from the dead and was seen walking around? My advice... follow the living, not the dead. And for those of you that are saying "I can't believe in a God who would send me to Hell," I agree. I can't either. But God doesn't send you to Hell. He created it for Satan and the fallen angels. You have a choice, and by not choosing to be with God through His son, Jesus, you chose an afterlife and eternity without God in a location called Hell. So essentially, it's your call; and if you don't make it now, then when? I advise you not to put off this decision, but if you do, remember that when all hell starts to break lose, and it will, do yourself and your soul a great favor and call upon the Lord's name in your final remaining moments.

It says in the Bible that there an army of 300 million men will cross from the East over dry land on the Euphrates River. The Euphrates River is drying up now and China has boasted an Army of 300 million men. But why would they go there? OIL! Israel just found the largest stash of oil under their country and everyone and their Muslim and infidel brother want it. You must have millions of gallons of oil to run jets, aircraft carriers, nuclear subs, tanks, bombers, ISIS Toyota trucks...oops scratch that- ISIS uses our Humvees and military tanks since Obama and Hillary sold it to them. That is why the butchers of Benghazi had to cover up the evidence and kill our ambassador because he found that out. Naturally, this will lead to Armageddon. By the way, there is a giant asteroid that even

Russian scientists have found that is due to slam into our planet; Bible calls it wormwood. Sounds like a movie with the exception that Bruce Willis will not get to save all humanity this time. That job is reserved for the Son of God and He will return. But this time, not gentle and sweet. He's gonna be pissed off and sort out some crazy and nasty globalists who have been making our lives, and our families lives, a nightmare. They will end up living in a real Hell. I hope you take this serious.

The reason I was able to write this book, go through so many near death experiences, save other people's lives, get off the crack pipe, be delivered from alcohol and a life of crime and much more, is because I did something that I hope and pray you will do. Time is short and life is precious. I want you to consider where you will end up at the end of your life. Even tomorrow is not promised; anything could happen at any second. The world is not going to suddenly turn everything around and have us all drive Priuses with rainbows and butterflies flying out of Al Gore's butt to save us from all the global warming bullshit. This is real talk. Ask yourself what your eternal plans are. I hope to meet you all in person at a book signing, or at movie releases or interviews. But if I don't or can't, I hope to see you in Heaven; and the only way that will happen is simple. Just repent of your sins and all the bad that you have done, and ask Jesus to be your Lord and Savior. His blood has already paid for our debt of sin. He has already picked up the tab on all our bad and is your defending attorney on judgement day in front of God. It's a really simple, free and easy thing to do, and once you've done it, you will feel such peace; a peace that surpasses all understanding. I feel like I have talked to each of you individually through the duration of this book, so with much love and respect, God bless you and your families. Stay safe. Stay ready. Hope to see you on the other side in Heaven. It's gonna be a heck of a party.

Andre "Relentless" Alexsen

John 3:16

Lightning Source UK Ltd.
Milton Keynes UK
UKHW01f1833110718

325576UK00008B/155/P